American Woman

The Poll Dance:
Women and Voting

Kimberley A. Johnson

Acknowledgements

A huge thank you to my mom and business partner, Ann Werner, for supporting and believing in me and for her unflagging efforts to produce this book

Thank you to my dad, Ken Johnson, for some great chapter ideas and for always being there for me.

Once again, Ralph Faust has produced a great cover. He always comes through. His expertise and creativity are appreciated beyond measure.

A special thank you to my readers: Jan Grape, Wendy Cartwright and Laura Stroube Hughes, who took the time to read this book before publication. Their edits and input proved to be invaluable.

Thank you to Samuel Warde for giving me a platform to speak my mind and spread information on his blog, *Liberals Unite*. I am forever grateful for his kindness and friendship.

I would not have been able to write this without the help of my friends and activists who consistently provide me with knowledge, updates and inspiration. The women working to ratify the Equal Rights Amendment are the new suffragists whose only goal is to make America a better place. When we finally see constitutional equality, it will be, in part, because of their efforts. Frankly, there are so many people to thank, their names alone would fill a book. I am including the people I work with on regular basis: Wendy Cartwright, Jacqueline Nantier-Hopewell Alaina LaTourette, Jenni Siri, Jennifer Rao, Eileen Davis, Portia A. Boulger, Tammy Simkins, Andrea Miller, Cathy Kaelin, Luanne J. Smith, Candy Graham.

Several people contributed their personal stories and insights and I have included their names in the chapter titled Women Have A Message For You. I appreciate the time they took to share their views and add their voices. It has helped to make this a better book.

Thank you to my friends and followers on social media. I have learned so much from all the people who have become a daily part of my life on Facebook and I am forever grateful.

Thank you Jeff Stutsman for coming up with the second half of title of this book. "*The Poll Dance: Women and Voting*" is inspired and exactly what I wanted!

Last but definitely not least, a HUGE thank you to the folks who donated to my Indiegogo campaign—in no particular order:
Susan Emry, Kristen Olson, Henry Rollins, James E. Flynt, Linda Utley Mulligan, Virginia M. Witt, MD, Heather Ruseskas, Angela Goldman, Sarah DeFlon, Susan H. Wolfe, Anne Kerns, Steven Baratz, Stacey Barker, Kady Denell, Beth Myer, Pauline Barraza, Alice McPeak, Lana Crowley, Patricia George.

This book is dedicated to those who have worked tirelessly to achieve equality for all.

Table of Contents

"Deeds, not words."
Dr. Alice Paul

American Woman

Hey, you. American woman. Do you believe you are equal in the eyes of the law? If your answer is yes, you are WRONG!

While American women enjoy many rights and freedoms, one important right we lack is recognized constitutional gender equality. The Equal Rights Amendment (ERA) was never ratified.

"Equality of rights under the law shall not be denied or abridged by the United States or by any state on account of sex."

An amendment to the Constitution requires thirty-eight states to ratify it. The ERA was ratified by thirty-five states in the 1970s. Everyone believed it would pass until Phyllis Schlafly essentially killed it with her Stop ERA campaign. She lied; people believed the lies and the amendment languished. Congress imposed a deadline and that deadline EXPIRED in 1982.

The one and only amendment that would make gender discrimination a federal offense expired.

Voting is not only important but it is vital to a thriving democracy. If YOU want a guarantee of equality, YOU have to vote. Otherwise, someone else will be deciding your fate. Don't ask for equality. Demand it! Take it! It is YOUR birthright!

***

You are a woman in a modern world. You like to engage on social media sites such as Facebook and Twitter. Maybe you're married. Maybe you're single. Maybe you're a mom. Maybe you dream of having a family someday, or maybe you love being single. Basically, you're the average American woman.

Imagine this:

You post an article on Facebook about an abortion law you disagree with. In your post, you express outrage and your stance on abortion. Your employer feels differently and sees your post. You are called into the office and it is explained to you that your post is against your employer's moral code and you are fired. You try to defend your position but it falls on deaf ears. You're fired. No more paycheck. No more health benefits.

You're angry. You can't stop thinking about it. "They have NO RIGHT!!" You start researching and find you're not alone. Other women who worked for the same company have been fired because of content on their personal Facebook pages.

You get an idea. You decide that you will organize a group of women and you will all gather on public property close to where you used to work and peacefully protest.

Five of you hold your signs. You've alerted some radio stations and local TV media with the hope they will pick up your story. Within minutes the police show up and tell you that you must leave. You argue that you are on public property and you are breaking no laws. Before you even know what's happening, you are all being arrested and taken away in handcuffs.

You are stripped of your clothing and treated like a criminal. They throw you into a cold, dank cell and leave you with nothing but your thoughts. You're angry. You're scared. You're raging and you cannot BELIEVE the injustice! No one will listen to you and you haven't even broken the law.

How can this be happening?

As a form of protest, you decide to go on a hunger strike. Days pass. You haven't eaten anything. Prison doctors put you in a straitjacket and say you're mentally ill. They restrain you and force a large, cold, metal contraption in your mouth to keep it open, making your mouth bleed, and then they stick a long tube down your throat and into your stomach where they pour raw eggs. They do this to you time and again until you vomit blood.

Does this sound extreme to you? Do you think it's

something that would never happen? It DID happen to Alice Paul. In fact, worse things happened to Alice. She didn't post anything on her Facebook page because she was not protesting about free speech; she was picketing President Woodrow Wilson in 1917 so that women would have the right to vote. She broke no laws. All she wanted was equality: a Constitutional mandate guaranteeing the women in the United States the right to vote.

Alice Paul endured physical torture so you can vote today. Think about that. In 1920, the 19th Amendment was ratified into the Constitution, and because of Alice and her undying determination, women won the right to vote. There were many other women who fought alongside her and suffered greatly for your freedoms. Shouldn't the right to vote be granted to every citizen? Why should anyone ever have to fight and bleed for the right to vote?

No teacher of mine taught me about women's suffrage. I didn't learn about it in school. EVER. Did you? Why? Why didn't the schools I attended tell me about this? This is important history. The incredible and heroic efforts women made are by and large ignored. That's a shame and it makes me sad. Voting is critically important and it is essential to a thriving democracy. Why else would men (and some women) fight so hard to keep women from doing it—even now?

There is a wonderful movie starring Hilary Swank titled *Iron Jawed Angels* and it chronicles the efforts of Alice Paul and Lucy Burns. I urge you to watch it and educate yourself about the struggles women have endured to secure the right of American women to vote.

I want you to vote. In every election. No exceptions. If there were a clear path to make everyone want to vote, someone would have already discovered it. All I can do is offer my suggestions and analysis. You don't have to agree with me on every point, but I hope that it makes you want to learn more and get involved. This book is a combination of facts, events and my personal experiences. And a little bit of begging. Please vote! PLEASE?

Herstory

For many, the term "feminist" brings to mind the tired stereotype of angry women who don't shave their legs. Hey, sometimes I am angry. Sometimes, in the winter, I don't shave my legs. But what the hell does that have to do with feminism? It just means I am human and I experience emotions. And sometimes I don't feel like shaving. It isn't a political statement. I also like tank tops, open-toed sandals and skirts.

Some women do not embrace the term "feminist" and when they give a reason as to why they wish to distance themselves from the word, it is usually based on false information or the desire to keep women from true equality. In order to continue making progress in the women's movement, we need to embrace the term and remember the women who fought so hard for the rights we enjoy today.

I am a firm believer in feminism and the importance of the word. Some argue that the term should be replaced with humanist or equalist. But if we throw this term away, we diminish the efforts and battles of the women who came before us. They were proud feminists and we owe each and every one of them a large debt of gratitude.

***

Abigail Adams was the wife of John Adams, the first vice president and second president of the United States. Among other things, she is remembered for letters she wrote to her husband about governing and politics. Their letters were filled with intellectual conversations and provide first-hand accounts of the American Revolutionary War. In the late 1700s, Adams was an outspoken advocate for women's rights.

She fought for women's property rights and educational rights. She believed women are much more than marital companions to men. She felt women should be educated and recognized for their intellectual capabilities.

In March, 1776, she wrote a letter to her husband and the Continental Congress, requesting that they, "...remember the ladies, and be more generous and favorable to them than your ancestors. Do not put such unlimited power into the hands of the Husbands. Remember all Men would be tyrants if they could. If particular care and attention is not paid to the Ladies we are determined to foment a Rebellion, and will not hold ourselves bound by any Laws in which we have no voice, or Representation."[1]

Alice and The Waves Of Feminism

Dr. Alice Paul was born in 1885. She was a Quaker and a graduate of Swarthmore College. She went on to earn her Masters in Sociology from the University of Pennsylvania, a law degree from the Washington College of Law at American University and a Doctorate of Civil Laws from American University. In her day, women were best seen and not heard. She understood that women needed to demand the right to vote because asking for it was a useless endeavor. In the early 1900s, it was a controversial and revolutionary stance. She and other suffragists held banners that read, "We demand an amendment to the constitution of the United States enfranchising the women of the country."

Alice's fundraising skills helped her to build membership and support in the fight for the 19th Amendment. She recognized that, in order to get the president to take the notion of equal rights seriously, she needed to be organized, systematic and bold. She started the National Women's Party. Lucy Burns and other "proper," educated women stood and picketed the White House with signs demanding equality and they refused to stop until their goal was realized. These women were known as the "Silent Sentinels." They were mothers, married to professionals or were professionals themselves, and they were graduates of some of the more prestigious schools.

They were not extremists—though some might have argued they were. They illustrated that thinking women were serious about equality.[2]

The fight for women's suffrage and equality didn't begin with Alice Paul. The first wave of feminist activity began in the 19th and the early 20th centuries throughout the world—particularly in England, the United States and the Netherlands. It was propelled by white, middle class women.[3]

On July 19, 1848, the first gathering dedicated to women's rights in the United States was held in Seneca Falls, New York.[4] Some of the movers and shakers in the group included Lucretia Coffin Mott, Elizabeth Cady Stanton, Lucy Stone and Susan B. Anthony. Just like today, there were divisive issues within the feminist movement.

The most divisive issue was extending voting rights to newly freed slaves. This included women, and there were many women of color who made history and fought for the advancement of equal rights.

One famous black feminist was Harriet Tubman. After escaping slavery in 1849, she worked as an Underground Railroad conductor and led hundreds of slaves to freedom. This amazing woman made it her mission to rescue her own family from slavery, as well as rescuing and helping other slaves. She earned the nickname "Moses" because of her ability to lead. She was active during the Civil War, working as a nurse and a cook. Her strength, conviction and moxie led her to be an armed scout and spy! A SCOUT AND SPY! Tubman became the first woman to lead an armed expedition in the war. As a result, she liberated more than 700 hundred slaves in what was known as the Combahee River Raid. She fought for people of color and she fought for women's suffrage.[5]

Isabella Baumfree, a slave who changed her name to Sojourner Truth, was an abolitionist who also fought for women's rights. In May of 1851, Truth delivered a speech at the Ohio Women's Rights Convention. That speech was recorded by many observers and became known as "Ain't I A Woman." Interestingly, the phrase "Ain't I A Woman" was not in the original recorded speech. It was added twelve years later. Some argue that because Truth was from New York and her first language was Dutch, southern idiom would not have been a part of her speech pattern. Truth fought for civil rights and was an outspoken activist for all women. She criticized the abolitionist movement for excluding women, and openly expressed concern and argued that women, black and white, should be granted the right to vote and that the movement would be diminished if only black men achieved victory.[6]

These women lived such passionate and astonishing lives, and devoting one or two paragraphs to their achievements feels like a smack in the face and a punch in the gut to their memories. There is a tremendous amount of information online and in the library. I guarantee that if you take some time and read about what these women did for you and for the generations that followed them, you will not be able to stop reading and you will feel a debt. I know that when I found out what they sacrificed for me, the words that echoed through my mind were "I'm not worthy." I thought to myself, "What can I do?"

I don't have to make history. But I know that I can take actions that will serve as building blocks and add to the efforts of my warrior sisters and brothers. I am holding the torch they passed to me. I don't have to worry about helping women win the right to vote. Thankfully, that is a battle that has already been fought and won. But there are more battles in front of us and I need to be a part of the solution, otherwise I am part of the problem. The same goes for you.

Unless one takes a women's studies class in college, most people don't learn about what women went through so that all American women would have the right to vote in elections. It was no easy task! And it is definitely something that should be of focus in all high school curriculums.

***

The second wave of feminism began in the 1960s and was more diverse. It drew in women of color, although black women and gay women were not always included in enough of the organized groups that eventually become influential later in the Twentieth Century. That said, the '60s and '70s were definitely far more advanced when it pertained to race and sexual orientation.

Author and activist Betty Friedan wrote *The Feminine Mystique* in 1963. It was a game changer and launched the second wave of women's liberation. In 1957 Friedan was asked to conduct a survey of her former Smith College classmates. She found that many were unhappy and unsatisfied with their roles as mothers and housewives. Something was missing in their lives and many women blamed themselves, feeling something was wrong with them. The book became an instant sensation and it prompted a social revolution. It dispelled the myth that all women were content in their roles as homemakers.

Despite the immense popularity of *The Feminine Mystique*, there was blowback. Friedan's children were no longer welcome in carpools. She and her husband found they were no longer invited to dinner parties. Many were threatened by her findings and not ready to accept that women had more to offer the world than ironing hubby's boxers.

Friedan did a lot more than just write about gender confining roles. She pushed for women to have a greater role in politics. In 1966, she co-founded the National Organization for Women (NOW) and served as its first president. She was also a champion for abortion rights and established the National Association for the Repeal of Abortion Laws, known as NARAL Pro-Choice America.

Gloria Steinem, a feminist journalist, became nationally recognized as the leader and spokeswoman of the women's liberation movement. Once a columnist for *New York* magazine, she later co-founded *Ms.* Magazine. She was a fierce advocate for the Equal Rights Amendment.

Steinem wrote about subjects that, at the time, had not been covered in the mainstream media. Her fearless efforts to push societal boundaries earned her professional praise and a loyal legion of women who longed for equality. Like Friedan, Steinem questioned the prescribed role of women in American society and noted that a woman had to choose between a husband and a career.

One of her more famous articles was a 1963 exposé on the New York Playboy Club. Steinem went undercover as a scantily clad Playboy Bunny for her piece *"A Bunny's Tale,"* where she detailed how women were treated at the club.

Against her editor's suggestion, she wrote about having an abortion. Of course it was scandalous, but her candor about the very controversial subject helped introduce the idea that sometimes women need, and should have the right, to terminate a pregnancy. She expressed that having an abortion didn't make her feel like the bad person American culture told her she was.

She later tackled other important topics that were not covered by the media, such as domestic violence.

Steinem, Friedan and other prominent feminists created the National Women's Political Caucus in 1971, which worked on behalf of women's issues.

In November 2013, President Barack Obama awarded Steinem the Presidential Medal Of Freedom, the country's highest civilian honor, for her extraordinary achievements and efforts to advance women's rights.[7]

Shirley Chisholm made history in 1968 when she became the first black congresswoman to serve for seven terms. In 1969, she became one of the founding members of the Congressional Black Caucus. She made history again in 1972 when she was the first black woman to make a bid for the United States presidency and ran for the Democratic nomination. Because of Chisholm, black women were able to see with their own eyes that with hard work and effort, a black woman can achieve as much as a privileged white man. That is a BIG DEAL. It is still difficult for women of color, but she is proof that we need to fight for what we believe in because we CAN accomplish anything.[8]

***

The exact time when the third wave of feminism began is up for debate, but is often marked as starting in the early 1990s. The 1970s movement was uncharted territory for women's equality and even though gains were achieved, one problem that arose was the unexpected backlash to the idea that women could have it all. The third wave questioned the definitions of femininity as well as the over-emphasized experiences of upper and middle class white women. Third wave feminism is also considered by some to have brought back the idea that women could dress sexy, have cleavage and low necklines and still be taken seriously. Modern feminists say we can be girls and flirty AND have a brain. Additionally, third wave feminists are more inclusive and celebrate all sexual orientations, race, ethnicity, and cross boundaries of gender to include transgender.

Women like Oprah Winfrey and Madonna proved that men weren't the only ones who could create empires. Former Texas Governor Ann Richards (D), Vice Presidential nominee and House Representative Geraldine Ferraro (D), Former Senator and Secretary Of State Hillary Clinton (D) Senator Elizabeth Warren (D) and Senator Tammy Duckworth (D), have shown us that women can be taken seriously in the political realm and make a real difference. It isn't just Democratic women who have made enormous strides. Many Republican women have also paved the way for women in politics and business: Former Senator Olympia Snowe (R), Senator Susan Collins (R), former Secretary of State Condoleezza Rice (R) and former California gubernatorial candidate and present CEO of Hewlett-Packard, Meg Whitman (R). You don't have to like any of these women, but there's no denying they made an impact on your life. They made it easier to exist as a woman with a voice.

When I look at how feminism is presented today in the news and especially online, I see a good mix of remembering where we were and where we need to be. A new crop of women is emerging on the scene because of social media. With blogs, books, YouTube videos and sites dedicated to the women's movement, there is a variety of new media to be utilized and new faces are leading the way.

Some argue there is a fourth wave of feminism. I am one of them, and it started in January 2011, after the Tea Party politicians took office.

Girl Power

Social media has provided a platform where people from all over the world can engage and share information. The downside is that anyone can post anything, so it is up to each individual to make sure the information they see online is accurate. The upside is that Internet conversations are reaching the mainstream media. The discussions we are having online are being noticed by the major news and cable networks, which means the journalistic tables are turning. It means that We The People are starting to influence the national dialogue in a way that was never available to us before. I first noticed this in 2013.

A 14-year-old-girl by the name of Daisy Coleman reported being sexually assaulted by football jocks in her small town of Maryville, Missouri. After the report was filed, her family was victimized and harassed by people who lived in their community. Daisy received death threats and was called a slut and other derogatory names. The accused rapist's grandfather was a Republican politician and the case was dropped unexpectedly, causing some to believe there was political influence. Two years after the report was filed, the Colemans decided to move out of the small town and were in the process of selling their home that was standing empty. A local paper reported the house burned to the ground. I, as well as other political bloggers, wrote about the story and it quickly went viral. Not long after, MSNBC's Chris Hayes featured Daisy's story on his show, *All In,* with a panel of women. Their conversation mirrored the online discussions about rape. Even though the subject matter was sad, tragic and horrible, I was delighted to see that we are having an impact on how the news is being reported and that we are influencing the discussion.

Other young women are making national headlines and it is no doubt that popular Facebook pages, Twitter and other social media sites help to spread the word.

One very notable young woman is Malala Yousafzai from Pakistan. She is an advocate for education. Malala attended a school that her father, Ziauddin, founded.

The Taliban had been attacking girls' schools in the town of Swat. Malala spoke out against them in 2008, saying, "How dare the Taliban take away my basic right to an education." In 2009, she began blogging for the BBC about the Taliban's threats to deny her an education. She was eventually awarded Pakistan's National Youth Prize in 2011.

When Malala was just fourteen, she learned the Taliban had made death threats against her. On October 9, 2012, she was riding a bus home from school when a man came on board and demanded to know which girl was Malala. When her frightened friends looked her way, her identity was revealed and the man fired his gun, hitting Malala on the left side of her head. Two other girls were injured in the attack.

The incident resulted in a massive outpouring of support from all over the globe. Thankfully, she lived through the horrendous ordeal and when she was sixteen, she gave a speech at the United Nations and was nominated for the Nobel Peace Prize in 2013. She wrote her autobiography titled *I am Malala: The Girl Who Stood Up For Education and Was Shot by the Taliban*. To this day, the Taliban still considers her a target.

Another young woman who stood up against misogyny and the teaching of abstinence-only education is a West Virginia student by the name of Katelyn Campbell. When she was a senior in 2013, her high school featured a guest speaker, Pam Stenzel, who preaches the value of abstinence without suggesting any other kind of sex education. The problem Katelyn and other students at the school had with Stenzel's message was that it was a shaming message—slut shaming, to be exact. The students of George Washington High taped Stenzel and alleged she told them that if you take birth control, "your mother probably hates you."[1]

Campbell spoke out about it and refused to attend the mandatory assembly. As a result, she claimed her principal made veiled threats, suggesting he would report that she was a "backstabber" who had "bad character" to the college she was planning to attend that fall. Fortunately, Wellesley College became aware of her public battle and tweeted to Katelyn that they were looking forward to her attendance and alerting the world to the fact they were on her side.

Her story began locally and made its way through social media. Wellesley students created a petition showing support for Campbell. A Facebook page was created called "Friends of Katelyn Campbell" and she received support from people all over the nation.

I was one of many who reported on what was happening as she battled with her principal. In an effort to provide real world information about sex to teens who are only offered abstinence-only education, my mother and I decided to make our eBook version of *The Virgin Diaries* free for a few days on Amazon. Over six thousand people downloaded the book. We felt we had to do our part and if we could put truth into the hands of six thousand readers, then we had accomplished something important.

Without social media, these young women and their stories would have been contained to their small towns and perhaps only reported on in local papers and possibly covered by the local news. Bloggers now have the ability to make stories like these reach a much larger audience and on occasion, the mainstream media picks up those stories.

The Why

Here's the thing: People of all ages don't vote. 94 million Americans didn't vote in 2012. They don't pay attention to what's happening—and there is a lot happening as I write this that threaten your rights as a woman. People complain their vote doesn't count for anything. It does. It IS important. It's easier to focus on the things in your life that are more interesting or take your immediate attention, like school and friends and work. When I was in my early twenties, I paid ZERO attention to politics and I didn't vote. I was even a registered Republican because I didn't know the difference between the two parties.

I have strong opinions. I will share them and I expect some people will disagree with me. That's okay. I'm going to give you some facts and then present you with how I feel about them. If you feel differently and think I'm full of it, that's fine. My goal is not to try and make everyone like or agree with me but to get you *thinking* about these things and taking action. Action can simply mean you have a conversation with a friend, post a question or your thoughts on social media and see what kinds of reactions you get from others. In other words, be involved. My mind has been changed when something is pointed out to me in a way I never considered. I don't claim to have all the answers. **No. One. Does.** I ask that as you read this book, you keep yourself open to alternative ways of seeing an issue or topic.

We live in a volatile time where women's rights are being destroyed and eroded. There is a fight between an extreme conservative ideology and a progressive one. It is nasty and scary. I don't want for any woman of any age to have to go back and fight for what our forebears have already accomplished. Sadly, we are doing just that.

In this age of instant online communication, everyone is a critic—including me. As a political blogger, I often see critiques that aren't related to the actual piece. Obviously, I will be critiqued, and I realize some people might expect that I should be writing about what they think I should be writing about. I want to take a different approach than other feminist writers. I want this book to be my stamp on why every person, especially every woman, needs to participate in our democracy.

When I got the idea to write this book, I wanted to write something that might have piqued my interest when I was young and not at all interested in politics. I didn't always understand or care about who represented me on a state or federal level because I didn't really understand how they directly impacted my life. Now I do.

My political activism is primarily on the Internet and the computer, but occasionally I have the opportunity to speak at events. In addition to my political blogging, I cover topics like sex, virginity and body image. I manage many large public Facebook pages and Twitter accounts. I *live* online. I am liberal, but I like to stay up on conservative viewpoints because sometimes I see something from a different angle and it forces me to really think hard about what feels right to me. I also feel it is beneficial to understand the conservative point of view when I am either not well versed on a particular topic or if I don't have a strong opinion about it. Understanding different points of view helps me to form a stronger opinion of my own.

Our system is imperfect and there are problems with how it works. But it's all we have, and in order to achieve progress and find ways to improve it, we all need to participate. It's not going to fix itself. Think of America as if it were a family of five. When there are five of you, usually the majority wins. That's precisely why *compromise* is essential—everyone may not be in complete agreement, a discussion is had, all points of view are considered and acknowledged, a vote is taken and a decision is made. Some are happy with the results, some aren't. That's life. No one gets everything they want, but everyone gets something out of the deal.

I ask that you make the effort to approach my views with all of that in mind. Form your own opinion and be present in the discussion.

1968 – 2012: My Political Evolution

A feminist raised me.

My parents separated when I was three. It was 1972 and a civil rights revolution was happening. Women were fighting for liberation, and the way women were being portrayed in society was changing. Women who were in the midst of redesigning the American landscape overshadowed the homemaker. I had no real idea about what was happening. I heard the term "women's lib" and I saw commercials that said women were bringing home the bacon and frying it up in the pan, so in my mind, women were equal. My mother was a single mom who worked. She struggled but we always had dinner together in the evening and a very normal routine. When the sink was clogged, she fixed it. When the car needed oil, she replaced it. When we moved, and we moved A LOT, she set up the television and stereo. When we needed more money, she worked extra hard or took a second job. She is a smart over-achiever, so we also experienced times where, as a single working mother, she earned a nice living and we lived well. My life experience exposed me to a strong woman who never relied on anyone but herself. She made sure to drive that message home so that it was ingrained. She succeeded.

I am extremely fortunate that my father is also pro-women's rights. He eventually remarried and my stepmother, Roz, is also a feminist. She believes in equality and is an Emmy award-winning editor in the news business. She kicks ass in her chosen profession.

In 1979, my father, who was a cameraman for a local television news station in Philadelphia, got the opportunity to move up to network news. This meant he would live abroad for several years. He wound up living in Moscow, Russia. The Cold War was on and communism was going strong. My father asked if I would be interested in living with him in Russia for a year. I didn't want to. I was afraid and would have said no, but my mother and my aunt basically insisted. I am so glad they did because it was a once-in-a-lifetime experience. I got to see with my own eyes what it's like to live in a communist country. It totally pisses me off when Democrats are accused of being communist. It only illustrates that those who make that argument have no idea what they are talking about, so they just make stuff up, or they parrot what they've heard without investigating for themselves.

When I lived in Russia, I was twelve. My only experience was being a citizen of the United States. I remember taking on an arrogant attitude about the Russian people. They didn't have the freedom to decide where they would work. They didn't know about supermarkets that sold thousands of products. There was the bread store and the open-air market where farmers sold vegetables and meat. People were oppressed and depressed. It showed on their solemn faces and the long, cold, gray winters magnified the oppressive mood of the big communist country. As I lived there and learned about what communism really is, I understood that my attitude and my view of Russians was not accurate and I was judging them unfairly. But I digress.

I have always been very vocal about my opinion, and I enjoy a good debate. In my high school speech class, most of the boys, and even some of the girls, would roll their eyes when it was time for me to speak, and say "Oh no, here she goes..."

I did well in speech class and my teacher loved me because I challenged the other students. I loved being part of a discussion and even though I have strong opinions and a great big mouth, I invite new ideas and ways of thinking about things. That class made me aware of this and showed me that, as a young woman, my ideas and opinions had value.

Turning twenty-one was exciting for me. I was an adult in the eyes of the law and it was my time to figure out who I would be in the world. I didn't give much thought to the enormous fight that had taken place to legally secure my rights as a woman. I knew women fought for the rights and freedoms I enjoyed, and I knew that we had come a long way from the 1950s way of life. I took it all for granted. I felt like a powerful badass woman who could do anything. My mother's strength as a woman served me well. I chose how I wanted to earn a living, and I usually negotiated an above average wage. I never had any real reason to believe my rights would be repealed or restricted. If anything, I assumed they would expand.

In the 1980s we had conservative presidents for the entire decade. Ronald Reagan was president until 1988, and then conservative George H. W. Bush took over until 1992. At the time, I was not politically aware. I was a young adult and what I experienced was the American dream. I didn't become wealthy but I had opportunity and I knew it. The world was my oyster. I do remember hearing about the abortion issue now and then. Occasionally some anti-choice group made the news but it wasn't plastered all over the media like it is today. I lived in a very liberal state and utilized Planned Parenthood clinics when I didn't have insurance. Birth control was always extremely easy to acquire and there were a few different times in my life that I was on it. I felt free. I felt equal. I considered myself to be a proud American patriot. **I mistook being comfortable for being equal**.

In the 1990s it was more of the same. Life was good and I decided to pursue an acting career. My best friend at the time followed politics and I remember her going on about some politician named Bill Clinton. My father was working for the news division of a major American television network on Clinton's presidential campaign and he invited my friend and me out for dinner one evening when the campaign stopped in Los Angeles. We drove to the hotel in Santa Monica and happened to run into Bill Clinton while on the way to meeting my father. He came over to us to say hi and shook our hands and of course, he asked for our vote. I was impressed for about five minutes and then I was back to not giving a shit about any of it. I believe I was still a registered Republican. I honestly didn't even know what that meant and I didn't care. As mentioned, my girlfriend was a lot more politically aware than

I was and she helped to convince me I was a Democrat. I eventually changed my political affiliation and have voted in every election since I cast my first vote for William Jefferson Clinton.

While Clinton was president, the economy soared, life was great, and the biggest scandal was about his extramarital dalliance with Monica Lewinsky. I am certainly not advocating marital infidelity, but while conservatives were in a tizzy about his sex life, the country as a whole was doing well, so most people, at least most liberals, didn't really care. His private life was not negatively affecting the personal lives of citizens.

As time progressed and we headed into the year 2000, Clinton was finishing up his second term. Vice President Al Gore was the Democratic nominee and George W. Bush was the Republican candidate. I was thirty-two and knew my choice was Gore. I remember feeling worried when the race wasn't in the bag for my candidate. I didn't like what I was hearing from and about Bush, but I did give him the benefit of the doubt. My mother, who is very informed about politics, predicted almost everything that happened economically after Bush became president, and she was extremely worried as Election Day approached.

Election night was tense—very tense. Initially, the media called Gore as the winner. We all went to bed and woke up the next morning to a different story. They were saying Bush, not Gore, won Florida, and that changed the results. It quickly became evident that something wasn't right and the Florida hanging chad fiasco was the talk of the world. The little pieces of perforated paper that were hanging on to ballots after they were cast made the final count confusing and unclear. It was "too close to call" and came down to that one state—Florida— where George W. Bush's younger brother, Jeb, was the governor. Hmmmm.... Recounts started and stopped as the two parties argued about what standards applied. The nation was frozen. The world watched in anticipation for weeks. It felt like it was taking forever and nerves were wearing thin. The conservative Supreme Court stepped in and **decided** the election. Five of the nine justices decided the fate of this country. They decided in favor of Bush, and despite winning the popular vote, Gore conceded. He was worn out and wanted very much to pursue educating the world about climate change.

In its unsigned opinion, the Court explained that it had voted 5-4 to halt the Florida recount. The Court's reasoning was that continuing with the vote count would violate the Equal Protection Clause of the Fourteenth Amendment and pose the threat of irreparable harm to the petitioner, George W. Bush. The Court stipulated their decision regarding the 2000 election could not be cited as precedent.[1] To me, that says they knew what they were doing was political activism and not upholding the Constitution.

In April 2013, Justice Sandra Day O'Connor admitted she felt leaving the decision to the Supreme Court was a mistake. In an interview, she told the *Chicago Tribune* editorial department: "It took the case and decided it at a time when it was still a big election issue. Maybe the court should have said, 'We're not going to take it, goodbye.'" And she added, "Obviously the court did reach a decision and thought it had to reach a decision. It turned out the election authorities in Florida hadn't done a real good job there and kind of messed it up. And probably the Supreme Court added to the problem at the end of the day."

It's a little late now!!!!!

The decision made by our highest court was the start of my political awareness. I knew my mother was right when she talked about what was to come of a Bush presidency, but I secretly hoped she was being overly dramatic in her dire warnings about the economy. Not only was she accurate, it was worse than she predicted. We had a long ride before the shit started hitting the fan in a way that I would feel in my wallet. Bill Clinton, while not perfect, left the United States with a balanced budget and a surplus.[2] We were in excellent standing with the rest of the world, so the unraveling didn't happen overnight.

On September 10, 2001, I was in Manhattan visiting a friend and it was the last day of my vacation. My flight home departed from Newark airport in the late afternoon. I remember arriving at the airport and hearing about a fire in the terminal. My understanding was the fire was not threatening and was under control. I boarded the plane and we sat there for at least three hours. I was so pissed. Everyone was. The captain announced that anyone wishing to get off of the plane would be able to catch a flight the following day, September 11, at no charge. I seriously considered it. I weighed the options and decided I would wait it out. Not long after, we got clearance and I arrived home safe and sound.

I was awakened the following morning by a phone call from a friend who wasn't sure what day I was supposed to fly home. She saw the attacks on television and was worried I was still in New York. I happened to be spending the night at my mother's house, and my mom and I watched with the rest of the world as the Twin Towers of the World Trade Center burned and collapsed and changed America forever.

Within two years, the United States invaded Iraq. The Bush administration was busy at work convincing Americans that Iraq had weapons of mass destruction. It has since been proven there were **no weapons,** but an agenda was being played out at the cost of the American taxpayer and, most importantly, American troops. FOX "News" was growing in popularity. Conservative politicians and pundits used fear to justify the wars and the spending. We were often on high terrorist alert—interestingly, the terrorist alerts would coincide with events that certain politicians didn't want the American people to focus on. For example, Homeland Security Secretary Tom Ridge claimed in his book, *The Test Of Our Times*, that he was pressured to raise the terrorist alert right before the 2004 election. Democrats accused Republicans of using terrorist alerts as distractions. Republicans deny it. But answer this question: How many terror alerts have you witnessed since 2009?

The housing market crashed in September 2008 and took the economy with it. It was bad. Banks had been lending money left and right to homebuyers, and mortgage bankers were making a financial killing—and killing the middle class in the process. To this day, these predatory lenders have not been held accountable. I had a friend who was just starting to earn upwards of $50 thousand a month as a mortgage banker in

2007 after only being in the business for less than a year. That speaks volumes.

Democratic Senator Elizabeth Warren of Massachusetts, who was elected in 2012, is fighting like crazy to bring the architects of the financial collapse to justice. She is a refreshing voice of reason in a sea of corrupt, lazy lawmakers.

When Ronald Reagan was president, he ended the New Deal restrictions on mortgage lending[3], making it easier for families to purchase homes with little money down. When George W. Bush was in office, the greedy mortgage bankers lent money to people who were unable to pay back loans and we saw the housing bubble burst.

September 2008 also introduced the world to Alaska Governor Sarah Palin—cue the dramatic nightmare music. I was absolutely not voting for McCain. I understood that he was a rogue Republican and had been admired for standing up for his beliefs, even if it went against his own party. That is admirable, but I still didn't want him to be president. He wasn't doing well in the polls and needed a surge of excitement. A YouTube search provided what the Republican strategists thought was their golden ticket. Sarah Palin is an attractive, conservative woman who was never fully vetted: a charismatic woman who captivated the world—for about thirty minutes. I knew from the moment she stepped onto the stage of the Republican National Convention that she was trouble. I felt a knot in my stomach as she outshined McCain and took America by storm. I immediately went online and started searching for more information about her and it didn't take long for the skeletons to come bursting out of her closet. The first story I remember reading had to do with her pregnant teenage daughter, Bristol. Personally, I don't judge Sarah for this. Teens have sex and get pregnant. But I knew it would be scandalous, and it was. That was just the tip of the iceberg. It became one scandal after another. I remember thinking that Americans love to put celebrities—and she was one—on pedestals, only to swiftly knock them off, but was there enough time? Would she be a heartbeat away from the presidency before Americans saw how dangerous she is? I was very worried. She scared the shit out of me. Would she mess up so drastically that the voters would make the best choice? In the end, she did. She was a train wreck that veered off the tracks in the nick of time.

Sarah Palin is an empty dress who was and is after fame and fortune. It was evident in her demeanor. A number of mainstream media interviews revealed that the governor, who eventually quit halfway through her term, didn't have the intelligence to effectively serve as vice president of the United States of America. She has proven to be an extremist nut-job who claims she's the real deal when it comes to patriotism, and us city folk are nothing but a bunch of freeloading moochers. Yeah, I kinda can't stand her. But Lord knows, I'm not alone.

I live in California, a Democratic (blue) state. It's pretty much a given that California will always vote blue. This makes no difference to me when I vote. I knew my state would go for Obama, but my vote is my voice and my voice was screaming NOOOOOOO SARAH PALIN.

Barack Obama won the election and the ugly underbelly of racism in this country was quickly exposed.

Just like we rode the wave of good fortune with Clinton's surplus, we entered the Obama presidency in the toughest financial times America has seen since the Great Depression. We are seeing a slow recovery but it's taking a very long time. Republicans don't like Obama and they absolutely will not cooperate. They fight against everything Democrats introduce. They have refused to bring the jobs bill up for a vote, voted no on the Affordable Care Act (ACA) and have wasted taxpayer money by voting more than fifty times to repeal it. They voted to stop unemployment benefit extensions for Americans who have lost their jobs and desperately need help. This is money that flows back into, and helps to stimulate, the economy. They have made deep cuts to food stamp programs and school lunch programs. They complain about President Obama's "out of control spending"—which is not even true (the spending has gone up far less rapidly under Obama than under Bush4)—and they cost American taxpayers $24 BILLION when they shut down the government in another ill-fated attempt to repeal the ACA. They have blocked progress on every front without offering any kind of plan of their own. The country is divided and the Tea Party has taken over the Republican Party.

Despite the fact that President Obama told everyone when he was elected in 2008 that it might take more than two terms to get the economy back on track, impatient Americans grew disenchanted and the 2010 midterm voter turnout was poor. Republicans gained a majority in the House of Representatives and Tea Party politicians immediately started going apeshit on women's rights. APESHIT! We are seeing the erosion of women's rights due to the passage of TRAP laws (Targeted Regulation of Abortion Providers) throughout the country, including extreme abortion bans and unnecessary transvaginal ultrasound probes. The worst part of it is that Republicans are refusing to debate with Democrats and are restricting access to women's health care. And even more unbelievable, in 2014, GOP politicians are attacking birth control. In fact, former presidential candidate Mike Huckabee said that Democrats are forcing women to be dependent on "Uncle Sugar" for birth control because they are unable to control their libidos.

In 2011 I was politically aware, but not acutely aware, of what was actually happening with women's rights. For the first year, much of what the Tea Party politicians were doing flew under the radar for people like me who weren't following the minute details. Slowly but surely, Planned Parenthood was losing funding. The chatter about the Susan B. Komen Foundation receiving pressure from Republican politicians to stop funding Planned Parenthood was getting louder in the first three months of 2012. Mainstream media was reporting more and more stories about how birth control was becoming increasingly difficult to acquire and women's clinics were unable to keep their doors open.

And then Rush Limbaugh opened his big, fat mouth.

When I Became A Slut

In February 2012, toxic radio personality Rush Limbaugh launched a three-day attack on a young woman named Sandra Fluke. Fluke was a law student who testified before Congress and eloquently made the argument that religious colleges should cover birth control in their insurance plans. She explained that her school—Georgetown University—did not cover birth control. She shared a story of a gay classmate who suffered from Polycystic Ovarian Syndrome (POS). Birth control pills are used to treat POS by preventing cysts from growing. Since the college did not cover oral contraception, her friend was unable to afford the cost of treatment, and a cyst the size of a tennis ball grew on her ovary, landing her in the emergency room. Fluke was polite, well spoken and understated. This made Rush Limbaugh very upset. For three full days, he obsessed on air about Fluke. He said that when she talked to Congress, she asked for free birth control because she was having so much sex she couldn't afford it anymore. He asked, "What does that make her? A slut. A prostitute." He then went on to say he wanted to see her sex tape if he was forced to subsidize her birth control with his tax dollars. The blowhard lied. Flat out lied. His tax dollars **would not** be paying for an insurance company to cover the medication. He passed off his lunacy as "news" and called her horrible names. Women across the country were infuriated with his misogynistic comments. The attitude women took was: If Fluke is a slut for wanting birth control covered on her insurance plan, then I AM A SLUT TOO!!!!!

A few weeks later, I penned *An Open Letter To Rush*

Limbaugh From A Liberal Slut on my blog. It was sarcastic, snarky and at the end of the blog, I included a link to the song *"How Can I Miss You When You Won't Go Away?"* by Dan Hicks and His Hot Licks. It was a Sunday, just before dinner. At the time, I only had one Facebook page; I was not yet working on public political pages. I posted it on various liberal political Facebook pages on their "recent posts by others" sections. After I ate, I checked to see how many views the post got. I was expecting fifty or so. To my surprise and delight, in less than two hours my post had over three thousand hits. I had dozens of friend requests and the comments were pouring in. One of the more popular Facebook pages, Being Liberal, posted my blog and people loved it. It was a complete rush—no pun intended. A few days later, I was contacted by the political website *Addicting Info* and was asked if I was interested in being a contributor. I immediately said yes, even though I had never intended on writing for an established political blog. At the time, I was concentrating on collecting stories for a follow-up to my first book, *The Virgin Diaries,* and was also working on my body and self-image project. But it was an election season and I was interested in politics and wanted Obama to win a second term. This was an opportunity for me to do my part. Interestingly, my mother was already a contributor to *Addicting Info.* I stumbled on the blog in January 2012 and knew my mother would be a great fit for them and I encouraged her to apply. She was accepted. When the editor of the site asked if I wanted to write for them, I was thrilled!

Not too long after I started writing articles for *Addicting Info,* I continued to post my Limbaugh blog on various pages and happened upon one new Facebook page titled Rock The Slut Vote (RTSV). I posted my blog and went on my merry way. Several days later Susan McMillan Emry contacted me. She founded RTSV United because of Limbaugh and the Komen Foundation's de-funding of Planned Parenthood. Susan read my blog and asked if I would be the RTSV spokeswoman. She explained how she researched my background and was impressed that I am an author and liked that I had experience as an actress on *Days Of Our Lives.* She also liked that my letter to Limbaugh was written with humor, which was the same approach she was taking. Her goal was to inform, inspire and educate women and most importantly, get people to the voting booths. She was uncomfortable with public speaking and needed someone to be able to fulfill that role. At the same time, UniteWomen.org was busy organizing a nationwide march against the War On Women, and Susan wanted me to speak at the upcoming Sacramento event. Unite Women was also created from outrage due to Rush Limbaugh's asinine insults and the anti-woman legislation introduced by Republican legislators at both the state and federal levels. In fact, there were over one thousand pieces of legislation directly related to women's reproductive issues that the GOP tried to pass in just over a year. They wanted to de-fund Planned Parenthood (and they are still trying), take away your right to choose and make birth control more difficult to access. I accepted Susan's offer, with my parents' blessing and enthusiasm, and thus began my official role as a "Slut." I had no idea what I was in for, but I was excited to take the ride.

I knew I was taking a risk with the "slut" title, but if I was going to do it, I would do it 100 percent. For me, this meant diving in and taking on this War On Women full time. My articles were primarily focused on what was happening with each passing day of the election season in relation to women's rights. The GOP never failed to give me something to write about. In June 2012, Republicans in the Senate blocked the Paycheck Fairness Act by filibustering the bill. The legislation would have provided incentives for employers not to discriminate on the basis of gender. When President Obama took office, one of the first things he did was sign the Lilly Ledbetter Fair Pay Act into law. This ensures that a woman has an adequate window of time to sue her employer if she discovers pay discrimination. The Paycheck Fairness Act takes it even farther by helping to close loopholes in the Equal Pay Act of 1963 so that women have the time they need to find out if they are targets of discrimination. Stronger penalties are imposed on employers who are guilty of paying a woman less based on her gender.

Republican legislators in Kansas gave pharmacists the

right to deny a woman birth control and the morning after pill based on their religious and moral beliefs. In October 2012, *US News* reported that in twenty-four states, pharmacists have refused to sell birth control or the morning after pill to women after their doctor prescribed it to them.[1] A common misconception about the morning after pill is that is an abortion pill. It is not. It is emergency contraception and it prevents a woman from becoming pregnant.

Legislators in many states continue trying to de-fund Planned Parenthood clinics. They argue that the clinics are "abortion mills" and insist they don't want federal tax dollars to fund abortions. The truth is, federal tax money is not used to fund abortions and the clinics are not "mills." Abortions make up only three percent of the services they provide. The majority of what the clinics offer is preventive care: Pap smears, mammograms and general gynecological services for low-income women. The GOP is hell bent on closing them down, based on what they refer to as "Christian values." The separation of church and state is flat-out ignored by those who want to deny women their rights, freedoms and affordable health care; and worse, they do it in the name of patriotism.

The articles I wrote had a link to the RTSV page, and with every new article we gained many new followers. When I started at the beginning of April 2012, the page, which went up in March, had just over nine hundred likes. By Election Day, we had over 14,000. Men and women were fired up and they loved the way Susan and I kept them informed while making them laugh. We needed to laugh. The 2012 election was a real nail-biter for both sides, so the humor and sisterhood helped with our growing concern that Republicans might win, or even steal, the election.

After my first public speech ever, in Sacramento, RTSV was contacted by a woman who wrote for the conservative website *The Daily Caller*. She wanted to do a story on us when she saw the YouTube video of me raising hell at the Unite Women rally. Much to our surprise, the article was fair and unbiased. No judgment, just straight reporting. That was enough red meat for other conservative sites to take notice and they did their best to discredit our mission. They attempted to criticize us by calling us sluts. Apparently the irony was lost on them. Fortunately, they failed and their negative attention led to high profile, mainstream media reporting on RTSV, including ABC, *Time* and *Huffington Post*. I was even quoted on CNN. We celebrated the coverage and found supporters from all over the globe. Over twenty-five countries loved our message and our moxie. We received enormous support from the French.

August 2012 provided me with another incredibly exciting opportunity. The grass roots group, We Are Woman, organized a rally for women's rights in Washington D.C. at the Capitol building and I had the honor and privilege of being one of the many speakers. My father was able to attend and he watched with pride as I stood, nervous but excited, and addressed the women and men on the west lawn of the historic American landmark. In fact, prior to the event, he joked and told me he would wear a tank top that would read: My Eyes Are Up Here. My dad! Such a card! It was a day I will never forget and I owe a huge debt of gratitude to Susan Emry for affording me the opportunity to have that amazing experience.

It is easier for me to speak to a crowd of strangers and not have people I love in attendance. It doesn't stop me, but mentally, I am more comfortable. My father has spent his entire working life around politicos, so the fact that he was there, watching me, made me nervous. As I stood on the podium, he was the ONLY person I was aware of because he was running around the stage photographing me from every angle. I look back and laugh and can't help but feel such love and support from and for him. I have been asked to return to the west lawn and speak again at the next We Are Woman and ERA Action event on September 13, 2014. The focus is on the Equal Rights Amendment and voter's rights! Right up my alley! This time around, I am one of the core organizers of the event.

The day after I spoke at the Capitol building, a Republican congressman from Missouri running for reelection, Todd Akin, started a firestorm when he answered a question about abortion. In an interview, he was asked if he believed abortion was justified in the case of rape. His reply caused a whirlwind of anger and embarrassment to his own party. He said, "It seems to be, first of all, from what I understand from doctors, it's really rare. If it's a legitimate rape, the female body has ways to try to shut the whole thing down." So that was pretty stupid of him, but despite the uproar, Republicans didn't learn to shut the hell up about rape. Once the rape floodgates were open, the "Rape Dudes," as I lovingly referred to them, were unable to control themselves. The comments and statements coming from older, white males about rape and abortion were becoming a large part of the Tea Party messaging, despite the resistance they got from other GOP leaders. Just before the 2012 election, Richard Mourdock, a Republican running for a Senate seat, said that a pregnancy resulting from rape was "something that God intended." As horrifying as it was to witness the crazy Tea Party shoving their judgmental beliefs down our collective throats, I didn't want them to stop. They were digging their own graves. It was fantastic to see a Democratic woman, Claire McCaskill, beat out Todd Akin in the election. She wanted to run against Akin so badly—even before he made the rape comment—she funded advertising for him. And she won. Now THAT is the power of a woman!!!

Even in 2014, the GOP still hasn't learned how to appeal to women. They actually believe that as long as they don't use words like "rape," they will be okay in the midterm elections. It's so bad, the GOP have CLASSES. They have to take classes so they don't sound like misogynistic, knuckle-dragging Neanderthals. It isn't working because they are still talking about rape. Republican State Senator Dick Black (no, I'm not making the name up) withdrew his congressional candidacy in Virginia after he pissed off the country in 2014 with his statement that he "did not know how on earth you could validly get a conviction of a husband-wife rape, when they're living together, sleeping in the same bed, she's in a nightie, and so forth, there's no injury, there's no separation or anything."[2]

I've always been a liberal thinker and I've always voted Democrat, but it wasn't until Tea Party politicians gained power that I felt threatened as a woman by the conservative agenda.

One of the perks of being a liberal slut are the trolls: those Tea Party folks who feel threatened by the truth and the fact that we are brazen enough to claim the epithet and take the wind out of their sails. Much like when the early colonists wore the term "Yankee" as a badge of honor, we did the same with "Slut." I have been called all kinds of horrible names. I was called a "cunt" twice in one day. I was also called a "liberal, lesbian, baby-killing slut." Another favorite was when a woman on Twitter tweeted that I was "a disgrace to humanity." One of the best was when a man called me a "Champion of Evil." I always laugh when they call me a slut, though. The reason I consider it a perk is because I know we have a voice. I know our message is working. I am still called those names. Unfortunately though, all women—including conservative women— have to put up with this crap, especially when we are vocal about politics. I may not like the views of conservative women, but they are not cunts or sluts. It's just a ham-handed way to try to silence us, and to anyone who chooses to refer to women in this unsavory manner, I often send a link to the book *How to Win Friends And Influence People*, and when I get threatening or harassing emails, I threaten to expose the sender all over social media and that seems to quiet them.

Happily, I've also received very positive feedback from so many women and men, thanking me for being a voice for them. I even got an email from a college student who attends a school in a conservative state. She was raised liberal and finds it difficult to fit in. She told me she shows my articles to her professors as proof that women's rights are under attack. Her note made me feel incredible. It made being called nasty names soooooo worth it. I have never considered myself a journalist—I am just a woman on a mission to spread truth and hopefully impact and encourage voting. Statistics showed that single women had a huge impact on the 2012 election and, as we all know, Obama won. I'd like to believe that I had at least a small part to play in his victory.

***

Ahh, slut. Not a name I would have ever guessed I would take on. I have received a lot of criticism from people on both sides of the political fence. It's exhausting to constantly have to explain it. But I do because I feel it's important.

The most common complaint I get is, "It's degrading to identify yourself by that name. It justifies everyone referring to women this way." Here's what I think: When Jane Doe of Steubenville was raped and urinated on by members of the high school football team, other women and even the mainstream media blamed Jane, the victim. Young female friends of the jocks were tweeting to Jane Doe that she is a slut. **That** is degrading. That is women giving everyone else permission to slut shame and saying it's acceptable to behave this way. Like it or not, America still has a long way to go when it comes to sexuality and how women are perceived. The media shoves overt messages of sex in our faces all the time, yet we are expected to act like "ladies." When it comes to our daughters, our mothers, our sisters and girlfriends, well, that's a different story. If an unmarried woman likes sex, she is a slut. If a woman is promiscuous, it is perceived as a sinful way to be. It's not ladylike or "morally responsible." If a man likes sex and is promiscuous, he's just a healthy man—a stud! He has to spread his seed and do God's work! Cough-cough-double-standard-cough-cough. We all know this is bullshit but it is the way many ~~judgmental assholes~~ Americans think.

My sex life is MY business. Not yours. If I choose to have sex with a different man every night of the week, it's none of your beeswax. If you believe a woman who sleeps around is a slut, *you* are the one with the problem.

The Anti-Feminist

Just because a woman is strong, successful or powerful doesn't mean she is a feminist. It means she utilizes and enjoys the road that feminists paved for her, and if she uses that road to degrade and minimize the hard work it took to build, she is not a feminist.

Merriam-Webster's definition of feminism:
1. the theory of political, economic and social equality of the sexes.
2. organized activity on behalf of women's rights and interests.

There are a lot of women in America who are for women's rights but say they don't identify as feminists. Others just flat out preach being submissive to men and they shame women who are not. There are those who say women who like sex are slutty and not pure. They believe women should "act like women,"—whatever that means—and "be true to our feminine nature." If we are not, men won't marry us. Being feminine and being a feminist are not the same thing, however they are not mutually exclusive. According to many of these women, liberal feminists are destroying the country. Yeppers ladies, the fact that we believe we deserve equal pay for equal work and want to control when and if we get pregnant makes us in-house American terrorists to these anti-woman women.

Queen anti-feminist Phyllis Schlafly DESTROYED the push towards equality for women in America. With her clean-cut conservative propaganda, she convinced vulnerable and uneducated women that if the Equal Rights Amendment were ratified—which it wasn't and still isn't, thanks largely to her—we'd see unisex bathrooms. THE HORROR! Women would have to fight in wars and widows would not receive spousal benefits. Basically she lied about spousal benefits—that has NOTHING to do with equality. Women are not yet recognized as equals in the Constitution, however there *are* unisex bathrooms and women *DO* fight in wars. Pamphlets were distributed warning women they would be eligible for the draft. Women in North Carolina who feared this wore pins that said, "All that is between me and the draft is the ERA."[1]

Schlafly warned that the ERA would hurt the family and would invalidate state laws that require a husband to support his wife. She successfully scared women into believing the best way to serve their country was to stay at home—to stay dependent and limited. You must remember that this was happening in the 1970s. We were just starting to see more and more equality, but there was a whole generation of women who were told that their only option was to be a wife and a mother. Many of these women had no work experience and limited formal education, so the thought of independence was frightening. Schlafly played on those fears and used lies to pressure women into fighting against progress.

Two very controversial issues were attached to the ERA: abortion and homosexuality. "The ERA will deprive state legislators of all power to stop or regulate abortions at any time during pregnancy. ERA will give women a 'constitutional' right to abortion on demand."[2]

Pamphlets circulated that claimed "The ERA will legalize homosexual marriages and permit such couples to adopt children and get tax and homestead benefits now given to husbands and wives."[3]

Schlafly is still worried about American women getting this amendment ratified because in May of 2014 she put out an urgent call to her followers to stop Illinois politicians from voting yes on ratification. She cited all the same threats she cited years ago. It's a pack of lies based on nothing. Here are a few of her lies followed by the truth:

1. ***ERA will require taxpayer funding of abortions.***
Not true. The ERA has nothing to do with reproductive rights. *Roe v. Wade* was a Supreme Court decision based on privacy. She used this argument in the '70s with success because the

issue of abortion was very divisive. It still is. She uses it as a fear tactic but it has no basis in reality.

2. *With the current attacks on religious liberties by the Obama Administration (such as the Hobby Lobby case), ERA raises the danger of denial of tax exemption and other discriminations against schools and hospitals run by religions that do not ordain women.*

Not true. ERA protects against gender discrimination and has nothing to do with religion or schools. Churches and other tax-exempt institutions are constitutionally protected and the ERA will not change that.

3. *ERA will deprive wives and widows of their "dependent wife" benefits in Social Security.*

Not true. Spouses will continue to receive survivor benefits when the other passes on. The beneficiary doesn't change. Conceivably, the term "husband" or "wife" will be changed to "spouse." Currently, both men and women can be beneficiaries of survivor benefits. The ERA has nothing to do with it.

4. *ERA will require young women to register for military service (even though we don't have a draft), and if they fail to register, they would lose their federal college grants and loans and would never be able to get a federal job. ERA will force the military to assign women involuntarily to ground combat in more "sex equal" numbers.*

Not true. Congress has ALWAYS had the ability to require women to register for military service. They have chosen not to. The fact is women have proven they are perfectly able to serve. If, at some future time, the draft is reinstituted, it will be an issue to be decided at that time, but it is safe to say we will never see a male-only military again. The ERA would actually help women in the military in many ways, and one of the most important ways it will help is a guarantee of equal pay.

The people who argue against this amendment try to play both sides of the fence by saying the ERA wouldn't change anything, so there is no need for it. Yet they turn around and lie about what it will change if it is ratified. You can't have it both ways. It either changes things or it doesn't.

We have come a long way since those tactics were considered frightening. Of course, there are still people who are afraid of homosexuals having the right to marry, but as a country, we are seeing more and more states legalizing gay marriage. Schlafly's threats fall on deaf ears and we can plainly see she was in it for power—quite a contradiction, wouldn't you say? A woman who dedicated her life to telling other women they should know their place, Schlafly traveled the country on her Stop ERA campaign, leaving her conservative family to fend for their own dinners while she promoted "family values." She wasn't being the good little wife who prepared the family meal and starched her husband's clothes. She cautioned that the feminist liberal agenda was evil and would lead to the destruction of the American family. She preached against the very freedoms she was enjoying while promoting her campaign of fear and lies. She enjoyed the road that was paved *for her* by FEMINISTS, the very people she was railing against. Her lies convinced enough people to defeat the massive movement to ratify the ERA. The hypocrisy of her actions and her messaging is astonishing.

As a feminist I am *supposed* to refrain from name-calling. I am *supposed* to be supportive of all women, no matter their stance. Fuck. That. Shit. Schlafly is a horrible woman. She is a toxic gender traitor and an insult to all of humanity. She doesn't want *you* to be equal, but she sure as hell enjoyed all of the perks granted to her by the women who fought for *her* rights. No woman did more to destroy women's equality in America than that woman. To anyone who pooh-poohs feminism—even those women who say "I'm a humanist" or "I'm an equalist"—instead of identifying as a feminist, congratulate Schlafly for successfully brainwashing you into thinking feminism is a negative word. And just in case you are wondering, I have NO PROBLEM with humanists and equalists; I AM one. I just haven't bought into the crap argument about feminism. I guess you've realized that by now.

It is very difficult for me to remain civil where Schlafly is concerned. So much so, that I have deleted what I really wanted to say about her because she pisses me off SO MUCH! Just know I ripped her a new one before I erased it. It was epic.

She is old now, but even after she is an ugly memory, her bloodline goes on and she has younger relatives who are trying to fill her rather large, stinky shoes.

***

Anti-feminist Suzanne Venker, Schlafly's niece, accuses feminists—me—of having sex at "Hello." She has never met me, and for her to assume this about an entire group of women is completely ignorant and judgmental. By saying this, her intention is to shame women who enjoy casual sex with the underlying message that good women only have sex with their husbands. She wrote about this in a book and a column titled *The War On Men* where she attempts to make the argument that men are really the second-class citizens and women are not looking for equality, they are looking for revenge. She says that men have not changed much over time but women have changed dramatically. She says that women are angry, defensive and that we've pushed men off their pedestals and now men have nowhere to go. Awwww ... poor men. They are so oppressed by the evil feminazis.

Like her aunt, Venker claims women need to submit to their husbands. She attempts to convince the public that feminists want to be exactly like men, which is absurd. (I don't want to *be* a man or be *like* a man.) Her argument is that men and women are different and need to accept their roles. Yes, we are different. But we are EQUAL, and we should always be viewed as equals in the eyes of the law. ALWAYS! Where did she get the idea that she's the one to decide what the gender roles are anyway? Sadly, vulnerable women who are afraid to take responsibility for themselves and their lives will echo her message.

Venker makes shocking statements so people will buy her books. In other words, she's just trying to make a buck as a hypocrite. If you are thinking that I am doing the same, consider the fact that I advocate choice and equality and utilizing your critical thinking skills. I am not asking people to behave a certain way in their marriage or assume any kind of role. I say live your life the way you want to. Investigate many points of view and decide for YOURSELF.

Venker preaches the false narrative that unless you are a subservient wife, there is something wrong with you. She claims that feminists are destroying the American family and are responsible for the demise of the entire social structure of our country. She isn't finding any fault with men; according to her, men are the victims. She just likes to point her finger at those "You had me at hello" sex-crazed feminazis who are turning men into a bunch of wussies. And that DOESN'T EVEN MAKE SENSE! The argument that strong, independent women are turning men into weaklings or less than an "alpha-male" would mean that these men are not strong enough in the first place to make up their own minds about who they are. It implies that men are really subservient to women and completely malleable.

Every time you analyze an anti-feminist's argument, it quickly crumbles. This attitude is damaging enough when it comes from men, but when it comes from women, it takes on a completely different meaning. It always reminds me of a battered woman who stays with her abuser because on some level she feels she deserves it. Venker and the women who share her negative views about how and what women "should be" are a danger to all of us because they help to keep all American women from real equality.

She proclaimed, "You can't take your paycheck to bed with you." That was in an article where she told women to lean on their husbands for financial support. According to Venker, women need to stay at home to take care of the children and to be financially dependent on men. Here's what she neglects to mention: many households require TWO incomes just to meet the daily life needs such as food, utilities, clothes and shelter. Hubby may find himself out of a job and when the wife has no resumé, what the hell will they do? When a wife decides not to work, she forfeits the possibility of getting a good-paying job if something happens to her husband's job. She might get one, but if she has no work experience, odds are she will have to take a low-paying job or start at the ground level. This is a topic that should be discussed by every couple who decides to live together, get married and/or have children. Being responsible is extremely important, and each couple should decide what works for them individually. If a woman chooses not to work because that is WHAT SHE WANTS, the couple must realize any consequences they will be up against if the man loses his job. Conversely, the husband might be the one who chooses not to work. This is a private matter that is up to the individual couples to decide. Not Suzanne Venker. For her to make a blanket statement and proclaim that a woman should "know her place" and allow for the man to take care of the bills so she can shop is like a 1950s freaking nightmare.

Venker also doesn't take into account the death of a spouse. What if the husband dies and there is not enough savings or insurance to cover the family's expenses? Should the grieving widow just run out and find herself another cash cow with a penis and start from scratch? Wouldn't that make her slutty and dependent on a "Sugar Daddy?" See the conundrum?

I am offended when I am told to take a back seat to men. I am offended when I am told that men are, and should be, the sole providers of a family. I wasn't raised to believe this. I was raised with married family members who both worked—aunts and uncles, cousins, my dad and stepmom—all of them were couples where both people worked. No families were ruined. In fact, when my mom and dad were married, my mom didn't work. She was a homemaker and mom. They divorced because they married young and weren't really suited for each other. My father and stepmother married when I was nine. They are still happily married and have raised two successful children. My stepmom is a video editor for a large news organization. Her career certainly didn't ruin the family.

Before women were able to earn enough money to support themselves and before they had the ability to choose if and when they become mothers, they had very little choice. Prior to the sexual revolution, being a divorced woman carried with it a very negative stigma: one where a woman was no longer worth marrying because she was considered "damaged goods." Men dominated the work force and the jobs women had, like secretarial and waitress work, didn't provide enough income for women to live independently. Women were limited and forced to stay in marriages to men who were physically or emotionally abusive, unfaithful, or men to whom they simply no longer wanted to be married, because they were unable to provide for themselves and their children. When women stood up and demanded freedoms, like the right to vote, the right to earn as much as a man in the workplace and the right to choose whether or not to be a mom at any given time, we were labeled as angry and/or slutty. We still are. Every day. Because we can take a pill to prevent pregnancy, we are labeled as loose and painted as moochers who depend on the government for free birth control because of our out-of-control libidos.

Venker, like anyone, has the right to get on her soapbox and tell people how she believes they should live their lives. But make no mistake; she is not a friend to women's rights or equality. She makes a living selling lies about feminists.

***

Ann Coulter is a completely different kind of anti-feminist. Her messaging does not stem from a belief that all women should be obedient trophy wives. However, she has stated that her personal fantasy is that women's right to vote would be taken away. She is the author of books that are nasty and mean-spirited. Her sales approach is to go on news programs as a political pundit and make incendiary comments as a way to draw attention to her hateful books. An example is her guest appearance on HBO's *Real Time With Bill Maher*. Just weeks before the 2012 election, she accused Maher's entire liberal audience of being racist while she promoted her book *Demonic*. If you are not familiar with Coulters work, here is *Demonic's* description on Amazon:

"The demon is a mob, and the mob is demonic. The Democratic Party activates mobs, depends on mobs, coddles mobs, publicizes and celebrates mobs—it is the mob. Sweeping in its scope and relentless in its argument, Demonic explains the peculiarities of liberals as standard groupthink behavior. To understand mobs is to understand liberals."

Coulter gets attention by creating controversy with inflammatory statements. Her loyal followers, fueled by rage, reward her by buying her books. They allow her to keep going and have given her a place on the national stage. During Bill Clinton's speech at the 2012 Democratic National Convention, she tweeted, "To get Bill Clinton to speak at the convention, Obama had to agree to carry his bags." She also tweeted, "Clinton just impregnated Sandra Fluke backstage."

The irony is that these women are actually practicing a form of feminism, but they are hypocrites. All of them are outspoken and make money and achieve power because of what they have to say. It really begs the question: Why are they railing against the freedoms and rights they enjoy—the freedom and rights women before them fought so hard to secure for them? Money? Attention? Or true gender equality? You decide.

Anti-feminists are a strange phenomenon. Some of these women take a radical religious approach. Others just seem to come from a place of self-loathing or anger. Why else would women fight against their own progress as a gender? It's not a new phenomenon. There were leaders in the anti-suffrage movement in the 1900s who didn't want women to have the right to vote.

The one thing that lifts me up is the solidarity I *do* see among women who want to break through the barriers and who work together for today's women as well as for future generations. I know we will succeed and I remind myself that obstacles serve to reinforce the need to fight harder and stronger.

As a woman, you must decide how you define which rights and freedoms matter to you. Your decision is important, especially when you use your power and vote. Do you believe women should earn as much as men for doing the same work? If so, keep in mind that Republicans have blocked passage of the equal pay bill. Do you believe there should be laws in place that protect women from abusers? Do you believe you should be able to choose to terminate a pregnancy? What about if you were sexually assaulted and found yourself pregnant as a result? Do you believe legislators have the right to make laws that dictate you MUST GIVE BIRTH to the rapist's baby? And moreover, do you believe that the rapist should have the ability to sue you for custody and visitation? If the answer is no, then get busy and learn if your elected officials or lawmakers believe this. If they do, vote for the other candidate—the one who won't force women to go full term and have a baby they don't want or can't afford.

A record number of twenty women were elected to the Senate in November 2012 and this is a terrific start. Keep in mind that who we elect as president determines who gets appointed to the Supreme Court. The President nominates and the Senate votes. Remember, the Supreme Court DECIDED that George W. Bush would be President.

Women can be strong and equal and also love men. I am one of them. I don't love all men, and there are definitely some men I want to remove from Congress. Those men are against my equality, and I would rather elect a man or woman who realizes that no matter our gender, color or socio-economic background, we are all human beings who deserve the same opportunities. Being a strong, independent woman allows for the freedom to choose a mate based on desire, not necessity. The women who promote feminism as "evil" are negligent, irresponsible and are slowing down the process of equality for all. Don't be one of them, and don't allow them to have power because you don't feel like dealing with it. You will pay later and so will your children.

Religion And Women's Reproductive Rights

The First Amendment to the United States Constitution reads: "Congress shall make no law respecting an establishment of religion, or prohibiting the free exercise thereof; or abridging the freedom of speech, or of the press; or the right of the people peaceably to assemble, and to petition the government for a redress of grievances." That first sentence is key. **Religion.** According to the Constitution, no laws shall be made in the name of **religious beliefs**. America is a diverse country with many different nationalities and religions. We hear about the U.S. being a Christian nation and that is not factual. Our founding fathers were, for the most part, Deists. A quick search on *Wikipedia* provides a definition: "Deism is the belief that reason and observation of the natural world are sufficient to determine the existence of God, accompanied with the rejection of revelation and authority as a source of religious knowledge. Deism became more prominent in the 17th and 18th Centuries during the Age of Enlightenment—especially in Britain, France, Germany and America—among intellectuals raised as Christians who believed in one God, but found fault with organized religion and could not believe in supernatural events such as miracles, the inerrancy of scriptures, or the Trinity."[1]

Since the 2010 elections we have seen many legislators who attempted or succeeded in writing laws in the name of Christianity. They have always been around. In the 1960s it was the John Birch Society. In the late 1970s and through the '80s it was the Moral Majority. These people follow a Christian philosophy, and their goal is to force their personal beliefs and agendas on to you and me whether we want them or not.

On June 13, 2012, Michigan State Representative Lisa Brown was banned from the House floor because she pissed off House Republicans when she was defending the right to choose. She used the word "vagina" and that is what got most of the attention, but what she said about her religion is very important and should not be discounted or ignored. She said, "Yesterday we heard the representative from Holland speak about freedom of religion. I'm Jewish. I keep Kosher in my home. I have two sets of dishes, one for meat and one for dairy and another two sets of dishes on top of that for Passover.

"Judaism believes that therapeutic abortions, namely abortions performed to save the life of the mother, are not only permissible but mandatory. The stage of pregnancy does not matter. Wherever there is a question of the life of the mother or that of the unborn child, Jewish law rules in favor of preserving the life of the mother. The status of the fetus as human life does not equal that of the mother. I have not asked you to adopt and adhere to my religious beliefs. Why are you asking me to adopt yours?

"And finally, Mr. Speaker, I'm flattered that you're all so interested in my vagina, but no means no."

Ohhhhhhhh SNAP!!! And for THIS she was thrown off the House floor!!! THROWN OFF!!! Would they have thrown her off for saying arm or leg? Would they have thrown out a male politician for saying penis? Lisa brings up a great point when she states that she doesn't ask anyone to adopt and adhere to her religious beliefs. But what if she did? What if Jewish politicians penned legislation that made it illegal to drive during Shabbat? Rush Limbaugh would have a brain aneurism. FOX "News" would implode. Shabbat is observed from a few minutes before sunset on Friday evening until the appearance of three stars in the sky on Saturday night. How do you think Americans would react to this kind of legislation? What if circumcision were mandatory? What if every male child was forced by law to be circumcised? It would be a law based on a religious belief and that is not what America is supposed to be about. The religious right would GO INSANE!

Before I go on, I don't wish to slam any one religion. There are those who practice quietly and there are extremists. The United States of America provides you with the freedom to believe or not believe whatever you wish. I understand how important that is. I lived in Communist Russia in 1981 and I met a group of people who sought refuge in the American Embassy because they were Pentecostals. At that time in Russia, religion was eliminated and replaced with universal atheism. The confiscation of religious assets was often based on accusations of illegal accumulation of wealth. The people of the U.S.S.R. were forced to live under what the government had decided was best for them. In this case it was the complete lack of religion.

Don't get me wrong: if you want to follow the rules of Christianity or any other religion, you are free to do so, because this country was founded on freedom of religion. However, we are also free to not believe in any religion. The United States of America is not a theocracy.

I believe in the right to choose, meaning I believe a woman should have the choice of an abortion if she wishes to terminate her pregnancy for any reason. I know this is an incredibly volatile issue that brings with it tension, anger and is often polarizing.

One conservative blogger wrote about abortion. Her argument is that it is legal and she saw no chance of that changing, and suggested that rather than spend time trying to make it illegal, opponents of choice should focus on what they could reasonably accomplish. Her feeling is that a fetal heartbeat can be detected in five weeks, and this is when she feels it should against the law to have an abortion. She believes abortion should be legal in cases of rape or if the mother's life is at risk. That is her bottom line. When I read that, I thought very hard and wondered if I agreed with her. The answer for me personally is no, I do not agree with her, but I also understand that she is using her platform to convince others of her argument and making an effort to change laws by using her power when she votes. We have the great fortune of free speech. We aren't arrested for our opinions, no matter how extreme they may or may not be. I don't believe her opinion on abortion is extreme; I just disagree with the details. Reading her take forced me to examine how I felt about the specifics. I was a bit wishy-washy on the 20-week debate, so I really thought about it. Should it be legal for a woman to have an abortion at 20 weeks? After carefully considering the question, I decided that no matter what, it should be the woman's choice as long as the fetus is in her body. There are some pro-choicers out there who would disagree with me. Opinions are like assholes. We all have one. What's yours? Do you know? Have you really thought about it? It is an important issue, especially when you're in the voting booth.

In the U.S., right now, there are states where there is only one remaining clinic that will provide abortion services. Mississippi is one of those states, and as I write this, that clinic is at risk of losing its license. The strategy is using TRAP laws to close down these clinics. The National Abortion Federation defines TRAP laws[2] as "Targeted Regulation of Abortion Providers." TRAP bills single out abortion providers for medically unnecessary, politically motivated state regulations. They can be divided into three general categories:

—a measure that singles out abortion providers for medically unnecessary regulations, standards, personnel qualifications, building and/or structural requirements.

—a politically motivated provision that needlessly addresses the licensing of abortion clinics and/or charges an exorbitant fee to register a clinic in the state; or

—a measure that unnecessarily regulates where abortions may be provided or designates abortion clinics as ambulatory surgical centers, outpatient care centers, or hospitals without medical justification.

TRAP laws often grant broad authority to a state's department of health to determine structural and staffing requirements for abortion clinics. TRAP bills discredit and burden abortion providers, and the goal is to chip away at abortion access under the facade of legitimate regulation. Abortion opponents introduce TRAP laws in an effort to say that abortion is an unsafe and unregulated procedure. When they imply that clinics are dangerous and in need of special regulation, they are being purposefully misleading and they promote the untrue fear that abortion is not safe. Abortion is, in fact, one of the safest medical procedures provided in the United States.[3]

The politicians who are creating, passing and enforcing TRAP laws to shut down clinics are Republicans. Democrats are not interested in making abortion more difficult. Religious views are often used to justify closing these clinics. Our Constitution specifically states that no laws shall be made to suit any particular religion, but people in Congress are getting away with it. The reason? Because those politicians were **voted** in. Actually in this case, the politicians gained seats because many liberals DID NOT VOTE in the 2010 midterm elections. A great number of people who voted for President Obama in 2008 were disgusted because the change they wanted didn't happen overnight, so they stayed home. Potential voters who believe religion has no place in government and who also believe abortion should be legal and safe, had a hissy fit and **chose not to vote.** In my opinion, that's a classic example of cutting off your nose to spite your face. And look what happened as a result.

If you have any kind of opinion about what your government is doing or not doing and you don't make an effort to vote, you automatically give your vote to the side you like least. Even if you don't identify yourself with a particular party, it is extremely important to understand what positions and actions both sides are taking on the issues that have a *direct effect on your everyday existence.* For example, if you agree more with liberals and Democrats and want the option of terminating a pregnancy, but don't feel it's worth it to vote, your choice not to vote is a win for Republicans, whether you like it or not. They may be the ones who will decide if you, or someone you know, can have access to abortion services. If *Roe v. Wade* is ever overturned, it will be by the Republicans. Their goal as a party is to erode the laws and eventually ban all choice, even in the circumstances of rape, incest and if a mother's life is at risk. They are not making any secret of this. Although the Republican platform has been anti-abortion in the past, it has only been since 2011 that we have seen extreme efforts to take away choice. Plenty of Republican women want that choice but are not always vocal about it. Furthermore, many of them have a tendency to vote for the candidates who want to take choice away.

***

Ever since I became an activist, I have been called many ugly names. Baby-killing whore is often hurled my way. My father jokes that I should put that phrase on a t-shirt. I've never been pregnant, so it follows that I have never had an abortion. There have been times in my life where if I had become pregnant, I believe I would have chosen to have an abortion. I can only imagine how it would have affected me. I'm an emotional woman and I believe that if I were ever faced with that difficult decision and chose to terminate the pregnancy, it would haunt me. I doubt I would feel guilt, but I would always wonder about what could have been. I know I would calculate birthdays, milestones and plenty of "what if" scenarios, but I also doubt that I would regret my choice. If I were to become a mother, I would want to be married to a man whom I trusted would be a great dad even if the marriage didn't work out. I would want to be able to afford to give my child a good life. I wouldn't expect nannies and mansions, just the feeling that I could provide the basic and necessary needs such as food, a good education, a happy home and love. As it turns out, I've never married and because I have chosen difficult careers, I have not ever felt financially stable enough to raise a child alone as a single mother. Now, in my forties, I am not interested in having children.

I assume the person who never met me, or has no idea what I am all about but calls me a baby-killing whore, was expressing disagreement with my belief that every woman should have the right to choose what is best for her and her body.

Women and some men worked very hard in the '60s and '70s to make abortions available, legal and safe, and for good reason. Women will have abortions—and get sick or die trying—whether they are legal or not. History proves this. Making it unavailable or illegal will not prevent it. Making abortion illegal is really about taking control away from women.

Does wanting all women to have choice make me a slut? No. And what the hell is a slut? It is basically a term used to shame a woman. The term slut is a social construct meant to undermine independence, freedom and confidence. It can be used to shame a woman who is sexually active, or a woman who likes sex. Maybe slut is used to make a woman feel badly that she wants to have reproductive choice and freedom. I've been called a whore, a cunt, a bitch and worse because certain people want to silence me and they are under some ridiculous impression that calling me a derogatory name will do the trick—or at least make me feel ashamed. So really, the word slut is just another way men and women seek to keep all women *in their place*. My reaction to them is an introduction to my middle finger. I refuse to allow anyone to define who I am with some four-letter word. And that is precisely why I embrace it. It has become common for me to refer to myself as a liberal slut. But make no mistake; there are PLENTY of conservative women who believe in choice of all kinds. These women also love sex. So the person who calls them a slut is just a sad example of a close-minded bigot. The ONLY way these derogatory and insulting terms can hurt you is to *allow* them to hurt you. The person who hurls a name at you is usually a fearful, judgmental person looking to make you feel ashamed of yourself so they can feel superior. Don't give them that power.

Slut shaming is real. I believe we will never do away with name-calling. Someone will always call someone else a name. It's human nature. There is a difference between using it to shame or to blame the victim if a woman is raped or using it in a way that is more of a slang term. For instance, on the sitcom *Friends*, the character of Rachel was going out for the evening and asked her friend, "Do I look slutty enough?" Does the use of the word slut offend me in this situation? No. Maybe it should, according to some feminists, but it doesn't.

Another way it can be used that is not offensive to me is when a friend calls you a slut because you got busy and told them about it. Gay men use the term—at least I have noticed this. So let's say I have been dating a guy and I finally do the deed with him. I may call my girlfriend or my gay man friend to share the juicy details, and my friend says in an encouraging way, "You're such a slut!!" Am I offended? Nope. If they say it in a judgmental way and imply I did something shameful, well, I can't imagine I would be friends with someone like that. I am not friends with anyone who wishes to shame me.

The point I am trying to make here is that it is all in the *way* the word slut is used. Using it to silence someone or shame them because they enjoy sex is wrong.

I guess it can be tricky. Some people are not at all comfortable with the word. Some are more relaxed about it. It all boils down to one thing: any attempt to make a person feel bad for enjoying sex is just completely LAME. Sex can be great—even if it's just for recreation and not for love. Just play responsibly.

Suffrage And Voting

What comes to your mind when you hear the words women's suffrage? If you are not familiar with the term, it sounds pretty negative. "Suffering" is what pops into my head, but that's not what it means. Women's suffrage is the right of women to vote and run for office. As I mentioned earlier, I don't remember studying the subject in school. Although I wasn't the most scholastic student, I had an excellent history teacher who managed to engage me, unlike so many others. Had women's history been taught, I would have been interested, particularly because of that teacher. I don't recall any other teachers or textbooks that addressed the subject during my entire high school education. I attended public schools in California. For those not aware, California public schools leave a lot to be desired. The last half of my sixth grade school year, I went to middle school in Maryland and spent seventh grade at the Anglo American School in Moscow, Russia. Although those two schools were definitely better with curriculum and discipline, I have no memory of learning about the long, hard journey women endured so that you and I have the option and the right to make our voices heard. That is wrong and is a crying shame. In fact, if you do a little research, you'll find most of "herstory" is not mentioned in schools unless one specifically takes classes that only focus on women's studies. This includes women artists, scientists, doctors and more. Did you know that the actress Hedy Lamarr was a pioneer in the field of wireless communication? When she wasn't busy being a glamorous movie star in the 1940s and '50s, she, along with co-inventor George Anthiel, developed a "secret communications system" to help combat the Nazis during World War II. The invention was patented in 1941, but it was ignored until decades later when it was used by the Navy in the Cuban Missile Crisis.[1] I didn't learn about Lamarr in school. I learned about her invention on Facebook. Women have been robbed of credit.

There is a video on YouTube where a young man tests college students' knowledge and asks them to sign a petition to end women's suffrage. Most of the students signed it without even questioning it. He asked them what they thought of suffrage and they would invariably say it was a negative thing. When I watched the video, I was disappointed. I realized I wasn't the only person who was robbed of herstory. I was also angry. This is not responsible, and it is a direct kick in the gut to anyone who has fought for women's rights.

As an admin for several different high-profile Facebook pages, the majority of what I post and talk about is politics, and women's issues are my priority. I see what builds a page and what people respond to positively, negatively and what they ignore. Sadly, suffrage posts are not very popular. A few likes. Maybe ten comments and some shares. Pictures of suffragists are usually black and white, and it's really difficult in today's fast-paced, colorful and shiny social media experience for people to get excited about serious looking women wearing old fashioned clothes in black and white photos. It's easy to overlook these kinds of posts when George Takei just posted a meme that says:

I got a dig bick.
You that read wrong.
You read that wrong too.

If you were scrolling down the news feed, which one would have more appeal? Which one would you click "like" on and which one would you share on your wall?

After the fight for the Equal Rights Amendment was lost in 1982, life went on. For several decades, women *felt* equal. In some instances, women earned as much as or more than men. It just wasn't guaranteed in the Constitution. Contraception and the right to choose became widely available and accepted. More and more, we saw government agencies and private companies instituting penalties for sexual discrimination and harassment. It wasn't until 2011 that the Republican Tea Party started attacking women's rights and when they did, they woke up sleeping feminist activists and created new ones. Like me!

I quickly realized that if I chose to stick my head in the sand and ignore what was (and still is) happening, I am part of the problem. Voting is vital, but sharing information is also extremely important.

Americans have a shameful record when it comes to showing up on voting day, and now the Supreme Court has opened the floodgates to make it even harder by essentially gutting the Voting Rights Act. Laws that once protected voters are gone and we saw many conservative states act quickly to enact restrictive voting laws that make it more difficult to vote. One example is the very red state of Texas. Part of a voter ID bill introduced by Republicans states that the name on your ID has to be identical to the name on the official list of registered voters. This poses a real problem, specifically for women, because perhaps a woman registered to vote before getting married. When she married, her ID changed and does not match the registered name. Unless she remembers to change over to her married name, she can and will be turned away at the polls. If she registered when she was married and she divorces and goes back to her maiden name, she has a problem and will be turned away when she wants to cast her ballot. If someone isn't aware of this law and waits until the last minute to vote, they will not have time to update their voter record and will miss the opportunity to have a say in the election. This is not lost on legislators who feel they can't win elections on their merits, so they use these sneaky tactics. A woman in Texas, who is a judge, had to sign an affidavit affirming she is who she says she is. It was in HER courthouse where she has voted for years. Everyone knew her. She was able to vote, but that vote wasn't counted for seven to ten days until it was verified as not fraudulent. It would be quite easy to "lose" that vote in the seven-day waiting period—especially when a certain party doesn't feel they can win based on their policies.

Voter fraud has been proven to be so rare that it has no significant outcome on an election. In fact, *Mother Jones* released an article in July 2012 titled *UFO Sightings Are More Common Than Voter Fraud*.[2] Here are two of the points made in the article:

- Only 48 percent of women have a birth certificate with their current legal name on it.
- Texas' ID law permits voters to use concealed-handgun licenses as proof of identity, but not state university IDs.

These ID laws not only hurt women, they hurt students, minorities and the elderly as well. Standing in line at the DMV means time away from work, and elderly people may not be able to get to the DMV on their own. These restrictions make it much harder to vote, and they are put in place for a reason—so people don't bother to vote.

Former Secretary of State Colin Powell, a "liberal" Republican, condemned the anti-voter bill in North Carolina signed into law in 2013 by Republican Governor Pat McCrory. In addition to requiring identification from voters at the polls, the law also cut back the time allotted for early voting and eliminated pre-registration for minors. Powell told an audience in Raleigh that he believes the restrictions unfairly target minority voters and ultimately hurt the Republican Party. He also said that the legislation will make it difficult for all individuals to vote.[3]

Powell said:

"You can say what you like, but there is no voter fraud. How can it be widespread and undetected?

"What it really says to the minority voters is ... We really are sort of punishing you."

In 2013 when the Supreme Court voted 5-4 to strike down the heart of the Voting Rights Act of 1965, nine states, mostly in the South, were able to change their election laws without having to get federal approval. This meant they were free to put into place discriminatory voter restrictions that adversely impacted minorities and women. And that is exactly what happened. These restrictions were put in place by Republicans because they know that minorities tend to vote Democrat.

If voting wasn't important or if your vote doesn't count, why do you think some people are scheming to keep you from the polls?

Why Vote?

In November 2013 the race was on for Virginia's Attorney General. The candidates were Democrat Mark Herring, who supports women's rights, and Republican Mark D. Obenshain. In 2009, Obenshain introduced a bill that would have required women to report their miscarriage to police within 24 hours or face jail time.[1] Herring won the election—by 165 votes.[2] In 2004, Washington State also experienced a close race for governor and it came down to 129 votes.[3]

Voting matters.

How do you feel about the 40-hour workweek? What about consumer protections or social security? Are you concerned about civil rights? All of these issues required a vote. Minimum wage, Medicare, worker's compensation and food assistance were all voted on.

It's easy to complain and blame politicians for legislation we don't like. It's easy to feel like your vote doesn't matter. I've heard it all. There are many arguments to be made for not voting, but they are really nothing more than excuses.

If you ran a company and one of your managers cost you money, brought down morale and did a poor job, would you throw your hands in the air and declare, "My employee is corrupt, so I choose to do nothing about it," or would you choose to warn or fire them?

YOU ARE THE GOVERNMENT. You hire politicians to serve you, not the other way around. The government is not some outside entity over which you have no control. If you believe that, you are wrong. Wrong. Wrong. Wrong. We all have a certain amount of individual power. Obviously, I can't just go and fire a senator I am unhappy with all by myself—much to my chagrin. I can't fire them on a random Tuesday in July. What *I can do* is pay attention to what they do during their time in office, and then I will decide how to vote in the next election. If you don't like how politicians are doing their jobs, you vote to FIRE THEM. Ignoring corrupt politicians only ensures more corruption.

Not only do your tax dollars provide them with a generous salary and comprehensive health care, elected officials are in positions to accept millions of dollars from corporate interest groups. What does that mean? Here is an example: Oil companies want tax breaks and subsidies (financial assistance to a company or a corporation) from the government. These companies will offer politicians money to facilitate their own interests and in turn, the politicians fight to get the company what is best for that company—not necessarily what is best for their constituents, the nation, or even the planet. The company gets money from the government and, in some cases, doesn't even have to pay federal taxes, even though their annual income may be in the billions. Think about that. Compare it to what you must pay in taxes. Each side is guilty of this, but where do you want your money to go? Either way, your money will be designated to subsidize someone. I would prefer to give that assistance to alternative energy companies such as solar and wind power, and I will vote for the people who will work to get us off of fossil fuels. If I choose not to vote, I give my power to the side that I like the least.

I asked some people on my Facebook page to give some reasons why we should vote, even if we don't like our options. The best answer came from a college professor of history. He said: "What I always tell my students: 'Will my vote make a difference? In the outcome of the election, probably not. So, why do I bother to vote? It matters ... it matters to me.' I would howl and fight if that right was taken away, so I darned well ought to exercise it on Election Day. It's the least I can do, literally, as a citizen in a democracy." I love that answer!

Here are a few more that I really liked:

"To forgo voting is a disrespect to those who have fought for the right to vote and the people who fought alongside of them."

"If you don't vote, you get the government you deserve."

"Not voting isn't a protest or a statement; it's a cop-out. A non-vote means you have given your power to the candidate or issue you dislike more."

"As a person who's been disenfranchised in the state of Missouri, I place high value on voting. There are few states that have a way for people that have no permanent residential address to vote. I was an over-the-road trucker, and had a UPS Store box for my mail and lived in the truck, as I only took off 2-4 days a month. The address was a business address and they denied me a registration. I went to the Voting Registrar's office to explain, and they encouraged me to commit voter fraud by using a friend's address! I told them all I wanted to do was vote in the presidential election. It didn't happen in 2008..."

"I consider voting to be a privilege. Great men risked being executed for treason to establish this country's independence and establish it as one of the world's first true democracies, with the citizens choosing their own leaders. The fact that 'great men' did it should inspire you to vote, as it was 150 years or so before women were granted this same privilege. YOU have the power to change the country!"

Another important consideration is the Supreme Court of the United States (SCOTUS). On March 27, 2013, the Supreme Court heard arguments to decide whether to allow gay people to marry. The decision was a victory for the LGBT (lesbian, gay, bisexual, and transgender) community. The justices ruled that Section Three of DOMA (Defense of Marriage Act), signed into law under Bill Clinton in 1996, was unconstitutional.

Section Three defined "spouse" and relating terms such as husband or wife, in a heterosexual marriage. Section Three codified non-recognition of same-sex marriage for all federal purposes—such as insurance or tax benefits. In other words, it did not allow gay couples to have the same benefits in marriage that straight couples receive. SCOTUS also shot down California's Proposition 8—which means California now recognizes same-sex marriage. The victory is a wedge in the door and paves the way for a federal ruling. If a gay couple marries in a state that recognizes same-sex marriage and then moves to a state that does not, they will not receive spousal benefits in that state. This WILL create problems for many couples and will more than likely result in a federal law that will allow everyone to be free to marry whomever they wish. It should be noted that Republican opponents to gay marriage have made asinine statements saying that gay marriage will lead to bestiality. Former Republican presidential candidate Rick Santorum was just one who made that ridiculous claim.

SCOTUS is made up of nine judges who are nominated by the President. **The Senate votes and decides who has a lifetime position in the highest court in the land**. A president who fulfills one or two terms may be nominating one or more justices. The President wasn't the one to decide whether or not gays have the right to marry or the right to spousal benefits. SCOTUS decided, just as they decided to rule in favor of *Roe v. Wade* in 1973, the women's right to terminate a pregnancy. When they make a ruling, it becomes federal law and that trumps any state law. For example, federal law says that marijuana use is illegal. Colorado and Washington have legalized the drug, but because federal has the upper hand, a person can still be arrested for smoking pot in Colorado or Washington if the administration in power decides to go after them.

Democratic presidents Bill Clinton and Barack Obama appointed liberal, female justices to the Supreme Court. Obama appointed Sonia Sotomayor and Elena Kagan, and Clinton appointed Ruth Bader Ginsburg. George W. Bush appointed Clarence Thomas, whose wife is an outspoken voice in the Tea Party. Bush also appointed the very conservative Chief Justice John Roberts. Perhaps the most conservative of them all, Justice Antonin Scalia, was appointed by ultra-conservative President Ronald Reagan.

Midterm voter turnout is usually pretty pathetic. It isn't as shiny and exciting as presidential elections. But the fact is, lawmakers have more direct control over our lives than the president does. State lawmakers decide individual state laws. U.S. Senators vote on and elect Supreme Court Justices. This is why it matters to you. This is why you need to vote in midterm elections. These laws and justices have a direct impact on your life. People who feel very differently than you about how things should be are voting. When you don't vote, you give them the advantage.

***

Have you ever not voted because you had no idea who the politicians were, and reading through the sample ballots made your eyes roll back in your head? If you answer yes, you're not alone. I hate those sample ballots. They don't give you the whole story and in the past, I have been left more confused after trying to get through one. When you decide to vote, you need to base your decision on the facts. You can't pick a candidate because they are attractive or your friends or family are voting for them. There are some people who cast their vote for those reasons. You also shouldn't vote on a proposition if you are not aware of all the pros and cons. The wording in the sample ballot may be confusing and it must be investigated further for you to make an informed decision.

It certainly isn't always fun to familiarize yourself with the senators, house representatives and all the local officials. It can be pretty boring, and sometimes intimidating. I admit I am not thrilled with it.

One fun way you can tackle this is by getting a group of friends together—this works great for college students. Assign politicians and propositions to the different members of the group. Each member will dig deeper and find out the details and keep notes. It is very important to research both sides, because even if you have made up your mind, your friend might hold different values and have different ideas, so find the arguments and the facts from both sides. Set a date where you will all meet to get together and discuss each measure and candidate. This takes away the pressure of you having to do all the work yourself and you can make a party out of it. Just save the drinking until after you're finished. Maybe you can have a potluck or you can decide to go out for dinner and drinks afterwards. You don't have to reveal how you will vote if you don't want to, and it doesn't have to be a partisan group. It would actually be beneficial to have people with varied views and opinions. This way, you can hear a side you might not have considered and when you keep your choice private, there is less of a chance of arguing. Politics, as you know, can get ugly.

One argument I hear as a reason not to vote is that all politicians are corrupt and that big money decides elections, so why bother? Well, to a degree, this is true. It wouldn't be true if 100 percent of the people voted. In the history of humanity, there has never been a system of governance that hasn't had some sort of corruption. People can be greedy. This is WHY we have rules, and voting is how you have your say. Wealthy people like the Koch brothers feed millions and millions of dollars to candidates and campaigns. An estimated $1 billion plus was spent in 2012 so that conservatives would win. But what happened? Democrats saw victories and President Obama was reelected. The money didn't work. I'll say it again. THE MONEY DIDN'T WORK. The corruption failed. That excuse not to vote is just that—an excuse. One can always find an excuse not to do something that requires effort. Does that make it right? Is that being responsible? Again, if your hypothetical employee were stealing money from your business, would you simply complain that employee is corrupt and do nothing because you don't feel like dealing with it?

Look at it like this: NOTHING will happen quickly. I don't care if you don't like it. I don't like it, but it *is* reality. Deal with it. We won't all of a sudden see immediate change. We never do. Change takes time. What we *can* do is slowly but surely elect the politicians who we feel will accomplish what needs to be done. We give them their shot at it and if they fail, we vote to fire them. We all have to realize that compromise is the only way to go because all of us will never agree on specifics. Never. Ever. We are people. We argue and disagree. We need to find the happy medium—which usually doesn't make everyone happy—but it is a way to satisfy enough of our collective needs. As time progresses and we continue to pay attention and hold these politicians accountable with our votes, they will notice. They want to get reelected, so they will listen to their constituents. We have made it way too easy for them by NOT voting. We elect them and then ignore what they do—until they do something that we don't like. A lot happens when we aren't paying attention. The result is often a rude awakening in the form of a law with which you vehemently disagree. **It's much easier to prevent something than to reverse it.**

I realize I am asking a lot. I am asking you to pay attention and be informed. I know it isn't all that exciting. I wasn't always informed about what was happening politically. But like a smoker, would you rather quit smoking before or after you get cancer? It's simple but never easy. It is never too late to get involved.

Sometimes it means holding your nose and voting for someone you are not thrilled with but who is better than the alternative. So, do it. Vote them in and then contact them regularly. Be relentless. Let them know if they wish to keep their seat the next time around, they are going to have to **earn your vote all over again.** Representatives have two-year terms. Senators have six years. Six years is a long time to be stuck with someone, so make your vote count. Eventually, if we do this together, we can have better options. Don't allow yourself to believe it is out of your control. And don't expect immediate results. BE PATIENT. Ignoring the leaky pipe only leads to a flood.

A parent who allows a two-year-old to run the show is being played, right? Parents are the ones in control. WE ARE THE PARENTS. Congress is the baby and we decide if they are going to keep working or if they go bye-bye.

***

Here is what people overlook or fail to see: everything happens in stages. We may elect a senator and that person may or may not fulfill their campaign promises. In fact, we are used to those promises being empty ones. This is because WE HAVE ALLOWED IT TO BE THIS WAY. Senator Elizabeth Warren (D-MA) is an example of a politician who kept her promise to go after the big banks. She is a politician who walks the walk. A rare bird. She is working FOR the people.

The flip side of that coin is Terry McAuliffe of Virginia. He ran against Ken Cuccinelli for Governor and won in 2013. Cuccinelli was against abortion and was very vocal about it. McAuliffe ran his campaign as a pro-choice Democrat who openly advertised his endorsements by reproductive rights organizations like NARAL Pro-Choice America and Planned Parenthood, an organization that spent $1 million on ads criticizing his opponent Cuccinelli. Shortly after the heated special election, McAuliffe reappointed William Hazel Jr. as his Health Secretary.[4] Hazel spoke at the very conservative Liberty University in opposition to the Affordable Care Act. Liberty's code of conduct imposes a $500 fine and thirty hours of disciplinary community service for students who have an abortion.

McAuliffe has betrayed voters. Most importantly, he betrayed women. It's the old bait and switch. Women are pissed. I am pissed. Ken Cuccinelli, in my humble opinion, is a lunatic. He obsessively tried to outlaw sodomy and oral sex.[5] And when I say "obsessively," I am not being dramatic or exaggerating. The dude had a major problem with people having sex the way they wanted. Knowing what I know about McAuliffe, I would still choose him over Cuccinelli. This was not my vote. This was Virginia's vote. But the idea is the same for all of the states. Virginia is a purple state and an important one. It represents what happens in politics in a big way BECAUSE it is purple. McAuliffe was the only choice for liberal Democrats. We now know his true colors and hopefully, voters will find a better alternative next time around. Perhaps voters will make enough noise so that McAuliffe will choose a different Health Secretary. They have the power to do that with pressure.

Can you see how the argument that politicians are corrupt is just a cop-out from your own responsibility?

I have already been asked by some activists to do an article on him and I may or may not, depending on my schedule. But here's what I DID. I tweeted to him and I posted an article detailing what is happening online. I will continue to follow this story and will make phone calls to his office. If I am asked where I live—so that they can ignore me when I say I live in California—I will tell them I write for a liberal blog and that first and foremost, I am an American woman and he has misled his constituents.

UPDATE

As I edit this book, the news continues to evolve and on May 12, 2014, many news outlets reported that McAuliffe is ordering a review of the medically unnecessary restrictions on abortion clinics in Virginia. He said, "I am concerned that the extreme and punitive regulations adopted last year jeopardize the ability of most women's health centers to keep their doors open and place in jeopardy the health and reproductive rights of Virginia women."[6]

I don't know what motivated him to do this. Maybe he felt some pressure. Maybe it was something he believed was important. In either case, I am happy he is looking out for women's reproductive rights.

Talking To Politicians

The world of social media has made it possible for anyone to have a conversation with politicians as long as they have email addresses, Facebook pages and Twitter accounts. In April of 2012, I had two interactions. One was a positive experience and one was very negative. And thus began my new way of reaching out to politicians.

My negative experience was with Republican Alabama State Senator Phil Williams. I received an email from a Facebook friend alerting me to the fact she tweeted to Williams. She told him that women were keeping an eye on HB57—a bill that tightens abortion restrictions. She included a link to a video that a group of women made in an effort to inform and make people aware of these restrictions. Williams tweeted back to her "Haha! Wait, was this serious?" She replied, "Yes!" He answered back "okay...for the record my wife and daughter say you don't speak for them." When I saw this exchange, I immediately thought "Oh no you di'int!" I wrote an article[1] about it and posted it all over Twitter and Facebook. The woman who emailed later informed me that the Senator wasn't finished mocking her, and he tweeted "...if liberals are not happy with my positions then I know I'm on the right track. Keep it up."

What a jerk!!! This man is supposed to be representing THE PEOPLE! I understand he has his political agenda, but for him to be RUDE to a voter in a public forum blew my mind. I replied to him and said, "There is a difference with unhappy liberals and you insulting women! #SenatorFail You will be in my next book." He countered with "Insults? So the vile tripe your folks tweet at me gets a response. Get over yourselves and learn to dialogue." I took screenshots of the conversation and posted them online. My hope was that if enough women see how he conducted himself in a public arena, they will vote for a more appropriate person to fulfill the duties of representing the people of Alabama.

A week prior to that exchange, I worked on an action alert for Progressive Democrats of America. The Illinois state website announced the ratification of the Equal Rights Amendment was up for a vote. I wrote about why we need the ERA. It was so exciting to be writing something that would be seen and considered by elected officials who would be voting. The vote was set to take place on April 16 and introduced by Democratic Representative Lou Lang. I work with the ERA Action Committee and all the women in the group were excited and made a concerted effort to spread the word. I wrote an article and noted that the majority of folks to be voting on this were Democrats and that we actually had a shot at getting it ratified. We all sat in front of our computers, posting in our Facebook group as we awaited the verdict. One of the women posted that it never came to a vote. What the hell???? What happened? We were confused and very disappointed. How can this be? We immediately started calling Lang's office. Evidently Lang's staff hadn't been versed in communicating politely with the public because as each of us called and reported our experience on the Facebook group wall, it came up time and again the staff was rude.

I called and a woman answered. I introduced myself and explained where I was from and that I was very disappointed the vote never went to the floor. The woman asked me where I got the information that it was supposed to be voted on. I answered that I work with ERA Action and had been following the developments. She told me that the information I had was wrong and suggested that we didn't know what we were doing. Clearly flustered, she raised her voice to me and asked why all these women were calling the office. I started to explain why when she shouted in the phone, "Why all the calls?" I honestly couldn't BELIEVE how she was reacting. I raised my voice and said, "Would you please stop yelling at me??" She hung up on me! I was floored! I called back because Oh. My. God! After several tries, another woman answered. We had a similar conversation sans the yelling. She pointed out that the ERA Action committee wasn't getting accurate information despite my efforts to inform her that it was posted on the state website. She asked where I was from and I told her "California." Her reply "Well, you're not even his constituent." Her tone implied that my concern was irrelevant. I reminded her that the ERA is a national issue. I was pissed. All of the activists were PISSED. I couldn't believe what had just transpired, and worse, that I wasn't the only one who had been treated so poorly. Although she is correct that I am not an Illinois voter, I AM a woman of the United States and the ERA impacts my life in a very personal way.

After I calmed myself, I wrote an email to Lou Lang, alerting him to the unprofessional conduct of his ill-informed staff, and I also let him know I have a very large social media reach. I told him the truth, that I have the ability to reach millions of people. I asked him why the vote never came to the floor and explained I would be writing an article and would like an official statement from him. I included my phone number. Within a half hour, I received a call from him. He was calling from his cell phone and he profusely apologized for his staff's behavior. He promised that he would talk with them to ensure something like this would not happen again. He then explained that he didn't know where we got this information, and we went round and round. I had screenshots of the Illinois website announcing the ERA vote was scheduled for 8:30 a.m. and he replied that just because something is posted to the schedule, it doesn't mean it will actually happen. Wow! Talk about misleading the public. Other women's organizations were keeping an eye on the vote that never was, including the National Organization for Women. He also assured me that although he has always been passionate about the ERA, he didn't have enough votes to support it, so he chose to wait and try to gain more support for the next time. He sounded very much like a politician when he told me all of this and I wasn't 100 percent convinced. The other women I work with weren't thrilled either. We stayed on him until he agreed to have a conference call with everyone in our committee, so we could get all of the details and work on a plan of action. I learned that I may have the opportunity to meet Mr. Lang at the 2014 We Are Woman rally. It appears he is sincere in his efforts to see the ERA ratified.

This may not sound like the most positive experience, but actually it is extremely positive. The fact that an elected official was so concerned I was going to tell everyone within my social media reach that he had failed to help women's equality and caused him to contact me in **less than an hour** after emailing him showed me that as a citizen, I have a lot of power. I may not have gotten exactly what I wanted, but Lou Lang is one of the good guys. He made an effort and he is truly fighting for women.

This is so exciting! Our ability to reach these folks and let them know we are watching proves they WILL make the effort because they want to be reelected. This is how a democracy is supposed to work. It was fun, thrilling, maddening, exciting and disappointing, and it is what America is about. PARTICIPATION—the people making sure the lawmakers listen to US!

I really hope you take a cue and join in on the fun. It's real easy. If you don't have a Twitter account, sign up! It's free and it's a great way to tell these people what you want. If enough of us do this, we will make it impossible for them to ignore us. But the keyword is "enough." One or two won't make a difference. Find out who is representing you in Washington. Find out who is representing you on the state level. See what they are doing and give them feedback. Call them. Email them. You may be surprised and you might get an answer! Always remember they work for you. You are the government and you employ them. When you believe it's the other way around, we all get screwed.

Contacting Elected Officials

When I began calling politicians, I felt nervous. I am not sure why I was, but I was. Truth be told, I would shake a little. I met a journalist who was also interested in writing about the

ERA. She revealed that she was nervous when she called a senator, so I am guessing many people feel intimidated. But like anything else, after you do it a few times, it's not scary at all. It eventually starts to feel empowering.

Most of the time, you speak with a young staffer and they don't usually know all of the bills you're calling about. It's great when they do, but don't count on it. I know not everyone will call, but even if ten percent of voters did this, it would make a HUGE difference.

If you don't already know, find out who your elected officials are. Focus on four offices: senators (each state has two senators representing it in Washington), representatives (each district has one representative in Washington), state senators and state representatives (one each per district, with the exception of Nebraska, which has one state senator per district and is a unicameral nonpartisan legislature). This is all easy to find online. Acquaint yourself with the people who hold those offices, no matter what their party. Once you collect their emails and phone numbers (state senators and representatives have local numbers and national senators and representatives have Washington D.C. numbers with a 202 area code, although they also have local offices), decide on one issue that you are concerned with. Pick something that either affects your wallet, your way of life, or the environment. For example, if you care about education and see your state has cut funding, figure out what YOU want. If you would like to see more money reserved for education, do a little online research so that you know your stuff and then formulate a fast and easy way to share your message. Two or three sentences will suffice. Write it out and have it in front of you when you call. Remember to always be polite. ALWAYS! It'll go something like this:

Staffer: Hello and thank you for calling Senator so and so.

You: Hello, my name is Jane and I am a (fill in with your state) resident. I am calling to urge Senator so and so to fund education and I would like for you to write down my message and repeat it to me after I finish."

Staffer: OK. (They are probably rolling their eyes now, but who cares? You pay their salaries.)

You: Slowly tell them your message and then say, okay, please repeat it.

Staffer: They repeat it.

You: Thank them, ask for an email address and tell them to have a nice day.

See? It's easy! Call all of them. It might take ten minutes. Then, email all of them the exact same message. Make a note on your calendar to do it again. Once a month is ideal, but even if it's only twice a year, IMAGINE what that would be like for the office if every day, people called at all times of the day, telling these tax-funded officials what the PEOPLE want them to do. Think of the effect it will have. They are NOT used to that. They ARE used to being ignored by their constituents, doing what they want and not having to answer to voters. They have their lovely health benefits, vacation time and, more than likely, money from corporations who want their agendas played out. If citizens took more of a participatory role in the laws we all have to live with, perhaps the corruption would lessen. They ALL want to be reelected. If they feel the heat, they will have no other choice than to do what the majority is calling for.

All that said, I realize it's a beautiful fantasy. I realize that in order to get people to act, they must be uncomfortable. So what makes YOU uncomfortable? Reproductive issues? Voting rights? Pick something. You don't have to be a full-blown activist, but do count yourself fortunate that you live in a country where you can have your say and the chips will fall where they fall. As always, be patient! Do not expect immediate results. I am fighting for the ratification of the ERA and I realize it may not happen for years. But I fight because one day it will happen and my part, as an individual, makes a difference.

It is paramount that you realize you won't always get your way and there will be disappointments. That is life. You keep trying. You don't ever give up. People have died for you to have the privilege of living in a country where the citizens have a say. We've gotten way off track. You will NEVER EVER be able to count on any of the politicians to make it better unless you lean on them and make your voice heard. THEY WORK FOR

AND SERVE YOU! Never forget that fact! You are the boss—one of many bosses. Take that job seriously for you, your neighbors, your children and those who come after you. It is activism.

"Activism is my rent for living on this planet." ~ Author and activist Alice Walker

Mad As Hell

"Equality of rights under the law shall not be denied or abridged by the United States or by any State on account of sex."

The Equal Rights Amendment was penned by Alice Paul in 1923. In the 1970s, the women's liberation movement led the charge to ratify the ERA into the Constitution. We got close. Thirty-eight states were needed and we had thirty-five. Phyllis Schlafly successfully halted the progress with the Stop ERA campaign, and the last three states we needed never signed on. A deadline was attached to the bill and in 1982, it appeared as if women lost the long fight. The deadline expired.

Think about that for a minute. Women's constitutional equality EXPIRED.

How does that make you feel?

Some people still fought, but the momentum was gone. Ronald Reagan was president and he preached and marketed a conservative America. It is interesting to note that it was the Republicans who originally introduced the bill. Equal rights for women has nothing to do with being Democrat or Republican. It's a civil rights issue. Period. Unfortunately, it has been associated with Democrats and liberals, despite the fact every woman and every person in America benefits when we are all constitutionally recognized as being equal.

There are always some people who will argue that it is not necessary to ratify the ERA. Some argue the 14th Amendment is all we need. The 14th Amendment was about granting full rights of citizenship to freed black males. The language of the amendment purposefully excluded women. Section two of the text uses the term "male" and "male citizens" three separate times in an explicit attempt to exclude women from the rights it intended to grant. The following is an except from the 14th Amendment:

(Emphasis mine) "Representatives shall be apportioned among the several states according to their respective numbers, counting the whole number of persons in each state, excluding Indians not taxed. But when the right to vote at any election for the choice of electors for President and Vice President of the United States, Representatives in Congress, the executive and judicial officers of a state, or the members of the legislature thereof, is denied to any of the **male inhabitants** of such state, being twenty-one years of age, and citizens of the United States, or in any way abridged, except for participation in rebellion, or other crime, the basis of representation therein shall be reduced in the proportion which the number of such **male citizens** shall bear to the whole number of **male citizens** twenty-one years of age in such state."

Keep in mind that the 19th Amendment provided women only the right to vote. Other than the right to vote, the exclusion of rights for women in the 14th Amendment has never been corrected—that correction would be a ratified Equal Rights Amendment.

Even the most conservative Supreme Court Justice, Antonin Scalia, said the 14th Amendment is not enough and commented the Constitution does not protect against gender discrimination.[1]

Supreme Court Justice Ruth Bader Ginsburg has this to say: "Every Constitution written since the end of World War II includes a provision that men and women are citizens of equal stature. Ours does not."

I work with a group of women who make up a number of grassroots coalitions, including We Are Woman, ERA Action, Women Matter Use Your Power and Progressive Democrats of America. In May of 2013, some of these women started a Facebook event called *I'm Mad As Hell*. They are Andrea Miller, Tammy Simkins, Luanne J. Smith, Cathy Kaelin, Eileen Davis, Candy Graham and Barbara Era Anderson. There are more women, and even some men, but this is the core group that I work with the most. And they do a great job. The goal is to remove the congressionally imposed (and EXPIRED) deadline so that we can get the last three states on board to get it ratified. We also want to get as many politicians as possible to make the ERA part of their campaign platform. If a senator, a representative or a governor says they are going to work to get the ERA ratified, more politicians will join them. Take marriage equality for example. When President Obama publicly supported it, it became the talk of the nation. The same can be said for equality for women. It is a nonpartisan issue.

When the ERA finally passes, no one party or gender benefits over another. We all win, including men. When you read the wording of the text, you see that no one is left out, and it does not even mention women specifically. It doesn't take any rights away from anyone. This means men are also guaranteed protection if they are victims of sexual or workplace discrimination. The most immediate benefit that would become federal law would be equal pay. There would no longer be a need for Congress to vote on whether or not women deserved equal pay. Kind of ridiculous that they do, and unfortunately, Republicans block it every time. In case you're thinking, "Boy, Kimberley sure likes to pick on Republicans," just wait. You'll see that this is one issue where I take no prisoners, regardless of party affiliation.

There is no valid argument against constitutional gender equality!

On May 9, 2013, Maryland Senator Ben Cardin introduced S.J. Res. 15, a resolution to remove the expired deadline, and House Representative Rob Andrews introduced the House version of the resolution, H.J. Res. 43. Andrews retired, which meant a new resolution needed to be introduced. The new one became H.J. Res. 113 and was introduced by House Rep. Jackie Speier on March 27, 2014. The goal is to get as many co-sponsors as possible so that it can be voted on in committee, showing significant congressional support, and eventually make its way through to the floor of Congress for debate. If it fails to go to committee, we must start from scratch in 2015 when we get a new Congress.

The ERA has been introduced every year since it expired in 1982. EVERY YEAR!

I consider myself an ERA activist. I help when I can by writing articles, tweeting and making phone calls. As I mentioned in the previous chapter, I realized that I was able to get the attention of Illinois Democrat Lou Lang when I informed him I would be exposing him for not introducing the ERA to the Judiciary Committee hearing in April of 2013. His swift reply to me via cell phone gave me an idea for the Mad As Hell campaign. As my fellow activists posted about their disappointment that a very liberal Democratic Senator from Virginia, Tim Kaine, was not co-sponsoring the bill to remove the deadline, I thought it was time for another threat to expose. Because the state is half red and half blue, the ERA fits in perfectly. There are plenty of Republican women who are fiscally conservative and socially liberal. If that is the case, Republican women can surely see the benefit of making equal pay a federal law—even the ones who say that pay inequality is a myth. What's wrong with solidifying it into the Constitution?

We were gathering support rather quickly and one was even a Republican (who later withdrew), but this Kaine dude was prime meat. So was Virginia's Democratic Senator Mark Warner. Virginia was a key state for the 2013 special election. It's part progressive and part Tea Party conservative.

The following is my diary of what transpired.

May 20, 2013.

After a few emails and phone calls to the offices of Kaine and Warner, I received a call from Kaine's Chief of Staff, Mike. I alerted him to the fact that I have a very large social media reach that continues to grow and that I write for a popular political blog. The goal was to single Virginia out. My deadline for the article was May 27. If I didn't receive any information, I would report that we are being ignored. We want official positions from these guys on the ERA. At first Mike told me I should be paying attention to what Senator Barbara Mikulski was doing for the ERA. "Oh?" I asked, "So rather than have a man support the ERA, you suggest we focus solely on the women to get this done?" "No, No..." he said. He sounded panicked and defensive and asked why I was threatening him. I explained I was not threatening *him*, I was simply asking for an answer and would report on whether we got one or not. I also informed the poor guy that if the answer is a non-answer, like we so often hear from politicians, I will make sure my readers are clued in. He promised to get back to me tomorrow.

It's a few hours after my phone call with Mike, Chief Of Staff. I feel really weird. I wonder if I have done the right thing. I am not used to being so aggressive and forceful. It's a bit unsettling but I know I have to be strong.

May 21, 2013.

Eileen called to alert me she and a few others would be meeting with someone from Kaine's office on the 22nd. She told me to expect a correspondence from Mike and he would probably be happy to tell me a meeting was taking place and he'd have more information for me on that day. Sure enough, a few hours later, I did get an email from him stating that he'd have something to tell me soon.

Senator Mark Warner has not responded to any of my emails or phone calls. I'll wait to see what we hear from Kaine before I continue to try to reach Warner. I figure if we get good news from Kaine, it will serve as a motivation for Warner to hop on the ERA train.

May 23, 2013

I woke up this morning to a voicemail from Tim Kaine's Chief of Staff. He told me that Kaine signed the resolution!!! That makes twenty-one senators who have signed on as co-sponsors! Eileen Davis, who likes to call herself the "Queen Bitch," was very happy to hear the news, as were all of my colleagues. I had a conversation with a staffer from Senator Warner's office as well and we are waiting to hear what he will do. Kaine's support showed us that we have some real power when we put the pressure on. After talking to Warner's office, I received a call from Eileen and she told me to focus on the California Democratic Senator Dianne Feinstein as well as Minnesota's Al Franken. I made an effort to let each of the staffers I talked to know that my goal is to report positive news. Of course, I let them know I will report the truth and if these senators choose to ignore the resolution, I'll write about that. In both calls, I was, once again, met with a little bit of a defensive attitude. I guess these folks aren't used to women standing up, taking names and kicking some ass. Tough. The Franken staffer was really worried that I would smear Franken. He asked that if Al doesn't sign within my deadline on May 27, that I point out all of the positive things he has done for women. He also wanted to let me know how busy Al is with other important pieces of legislation. I explained that women are important too, especially at voting time and we remember. He brought up The Violence Against Women Act and how Al had a lot to do with getting it passed recently. I let him know that I was fully aware of the VAWA but my article focused on the ERA, and that I would be letting my readers know what Al does or doesn't do regarding the resolution to remove the deadline. I pointed out that it would only take a few minutes of his time and I also pointed out that Franken's fellow Minnesota senator, Amy Klobuchar, signed the bill the previous day.

It's been an eventful day and quite exciting. Although my colleagues and I are only a small group of women, we do have a very large audience, and we are seeing democracy in action. When a citizen decides to make a difference and puts pressure on those who are working for us, we see results. It will take some time but I can't help thinking that if—when—this ERA deadline is removed, it shouldn't take too long to find three states to finally get this done. We've been waiting since 1923. It's about time!

May 27, 2013

It's Memorial Day. It appears that Senator Mark Warner of Virginia is ignoring all the phone calls, tweets and emails he is getting asking him to co-sponsor this damned resolution. Eileen and others visited his office last week and spoke to Nicholas, Warner's legislative aide. Nicholas suggested that we should just go ahead, get the last three states to ratify and THEN come back and ask that the deadline be removed.

Eileen explained to this person that we (The ERA) are in detention—expired deadline and all. Since Nicholas was fortunate enough to be born with a penis and doesn't have to fight for HIS right to be acknowledged in the Constitution, he doesn't really seem to give a shit that women are still looking for their equality. The equality that WE SHOULDN'T HAVE TO ASK FOR!!!! It's probably best I was not at this meeting. I might have called Nicholas a fuckbagel or a douchecanoe and ruined everything with my unladylike potty mouth. I sit here and type and wonder what the fuck??? It's 2013. Why are women still waiting to be granted equal rights? It's time to DEMAND equality—not ask for it!!! Why isn't Obama saying anything? Why isn't Michelle Obama saying anything?? To make matters worse, the old bag of skin who helped ruin progress for all U.S. women, Phyllis Schlafly, whose son is gay, recently spoke out against homosexuals and of course, she had to add how feminists have ruined the family. Oy. I am in a mood. Tomorrow the fight continues and I believe it's time to write an article about Warner. Maybe if he sees it, he'll do the right thing and sign.

June 6, 2013

The *Liberals Unite* article on Warner came out on June 3 and was titled *"Is Virginia Democratic Senator Mark Warner A Misogynist And Chauvinist?"* Everything was outlined. I noted that his staff was ignoring us and included a quote from Eileen Davis that Warner's legislative aide was nice but dismissive. Last night, Eileen received the email that Warner has agreed to sign on! It is unfortunate that it took an unflattering article to get Warner to step up but it worked!!! This is what happens when people actively participate in government. It proves that with a little effort, we can pressure our senators and representatives to act. If only everyone took advantage of their individual power and called their congressional representatives. The more people who recognize the power they wield, the better chance we have of achieving victory as a collective, majority voice.

The next senator who will be singled out is Al Franken. I personally love him and I do know he supports equality. I have been going back and forth on the phone and with emails to his staff and unfortunately, all I got was a pat on the head, and basically sent on my way. I received an email this morning from a staffer who informed me that Franken supports the ERA. Hey, that's great but it isn't enough. The goal here is to get him to sign the resolution that removes the deadline. When I spoke to this staffer on the phone, he was very clear that Franken is busy with the Farm Bill. I explained that a signature will only take a few minutes of his time. So I have now made it very clear that playtime is over. I sent him a copy of the Warner article and informed Franken's guy that they have until June 10. We mean business. I honestly hate doing this. I hate that some Democrats in power are refusing to make this a part of their platform. I hate that women are not yet guaranteed federal equality against discrimination. I hate that Democratic politicians are acting like wimps about getting this done! Until we see equality in the Constitution, I will continue to be the bad cop and call out every single one who is too damned lazy to get the ERA passed!

June 19, 2013

In just over one month, we have reached out to seventy representatives and twenty-five senators who have agreed to co-sponsor the resolution to remove the deadline from the ERA. I spoke to someone who asked to remain anonymous, so I will call this person Pat. Pat told me the article on Warner I wrote was not appreciated by certain politicians and evidently it caused some chatter in the halls of Congress. GOOD! Who the hell do these people think they are? They are not our bosses. They are public servants. Seriously, the *gall*! So, basically people are upset because I wrote an unflattering article about a man who was ignoring women. In the end, he felt the pressure and did the right thing. The ERA advocates I work with want equality and evidently, that makes us bitches. Yes, we've heard it before. Strong women are bitches. I guess the shoe fits. So I am now a slut *and* a bitch, YAY! Oh, let's not forget I'm also a baby-killing whore, but I digress.

Pat also informed me that Senator Richard Blumenthal of Connecticut was an important get as a co-sponsor. Frankly, I don't know why and it wasn't explained to me. I contacted his office a few weeks ago alerting his Chief of Staff that I am writing an article. I received no reply. Typical. I waited a few weeks and emailed her again. No reply. I emailed her again and then I posted on Facebook. I asked that people call his office and ask that he sponsor the resolution. Comments came in and the reports were that she was passing the information on to the Senator. This was yesterday. Today, I woke up to an email from Blumenthal's Director of Communications and it said that he is a co-sponsor. YES! VICTORY!

UPDATE: February 8, 2014.

The summer proved to be slow—at least where I was concerned. I still made calls and threatened various politicians with articles, and although I will never know if those who signed did so because of me, I do know that I was only one of many who helped secure the signatures. When we targeted someone, we all called and we all made an effort. I know I had some influence, but my efforts alone would not have seen as much success unless it was a group effort. The activists—my friends—dedicate so much more of their time than I can and when the ERA is finally ratified, the women I mention in this "diary" need to be recognized and remembered for the huge role they played. Most are not looking for notoriety. They just want equality realized.

***

In the beginning of 2014, I made the decision that I would stop writing unflattering articles about Democrats in this election year. There are a few reasons: the coming midterm elections are too important and the focus for progressives is to vote out Tea Party politicians. Although I have some influence, I don't have enough influence to make a solid difference either way. I don't want to be responsible for turning any Democratic voters away, and I also don't want my Internet following to turn on me. That saddens me but I understand it. I would prefer that we don't have to start from scratch in 2015.

The good news is that, despite the fact I am not dragging Democrats through the mud for a while, the women who are working hard so that women finally achieve full equality are making positive strides.

UPDATE: June 13, 2014

Senator Al Franken co-signed the resolution! It took a year but he did it! Several of the ERA activists stayed on him and eventually contact was made with a new female staffer. After explaining what S.J. Res. 15 is and detailing our plans to rally in Washington, we got word that he signed!

No one is going to give women the equality we deserve. They will only do it when we demand it. What are you waiting for?

Agitate.

Little Things DO Matter

In this chapter I am going to discuss the little things men say to women that chip away at our confidence and keep us from being and feeling equal. Before I do, I wish to point out a few things. Sometimes men say unfavorable things to women because that's what people do to each other. Men do it to other men and women do it to other women. It's important to not be overly sensitive and on the attack. Women friends of mine have said things to me that were meant as little digs. It's just human nature. As a feminist, I make an effort to be very careful about how I react, and I don't want to scream "misogyny" every time a man is an asshole. That would be extreme and unfair.

Women still have many obstacles to overcome: equality in the Constitution, being accused of asking to be raped due to their manner of dress, fair pay in the work place and equal representation in Congress, to name a few. Those are some big issues, but how do we deal with it when a man "puts us in our place?" Sometimes it's not easy to answer. I'll give you some examples of things men have said to me over the years and how I reacted.

I used to be a sales representative in a field dominated by blue-collar men. Many of these men were great. They treated me with respect and never once made me feel uncomfortable. There were also the men who had to show me who was boss. One man, "John," who was my employer, was giving me a lecture—after I had proven my worth at the company by selling a $30,000 machine to a water and power plant all on my own, with very little help from my male sales manager,

"Adam." I had only been employed by the company for a few months and was excited that I had made such a large and difficult sale, and asked John for more information on oil filtration so that I could sell more big-ticket items. He said yes and then he told me that in order to not be seen as a bimbo, I would need to understand what it was I was selling. I remember being shocked by his absurd, sexist remark.

Bimbo.

I didn't say anything to him about his "bimbo" comment because I needed to process it. As I drove home, I became increasingly irritated. I had already sold the damn machine—with NO HELP from him. My customers never treated me as if I were a bimbo. I asked this man for some more education so that I could hone my sales skills. Rather than praise, rather than a pat on the back for a job well done, I was loosely referred to as a bimbo. I took a risk and called him after I gathered myself and had a few good workouts where I mentally beat the shit out of him. I knew flying off the handle would be of no help and would give him the green light to call me overly emotional and unable to handle the job. This man was very much the alpha male—very macho. So I called him and simply addressed the situation calmly. I told him I understood that he didn't outright call me a bimbo, but his reference to the fact that I would be seen that way because I wasn't yet an expert in my field was insulting. I made the effort to make sure he understood that he was not ever permitted to address me in that way again, but I stayed centered, calm and measured. In that instance, it worked. He basically avoided me after our conversation. I embarrassed him. That wasn't my goal. My goal was to make him realize he had been a sexist employer. He apologized and even though I am sure my reaction didn't turn him into a feminist, it made ME feel better and more in control of my life, both personally and at work. If I had said nothing, it would have chipped away at me and possibly would have manifested into misplaced anger. I hope that it made him consider his words when speaking with his female employees. He isn't a bad man. But he did need a good reminder that he wasn't superior just because he has a penis.

Sometimes, it's not so easy to speak up in the workplace,

especially when it's a customer who is being demeaning. As mentioned, my customers were predominantly men and I heard some real doozies. One day I was sitting in a customer's office and we were having a perfectly nice chat. He had always been a gentleman in the past and we had a good working relationship. He felt comfortable talking with me—a little too comfortable. He launched into his story about his unfulfilling marriage—I'll bet you know where this is going. He told me that he had affairs. Here we go. I was pretty sure his reason for letting me in on his little secret was a way for him to let me know I could be one of his special lady friends. I sat there, trying not to appear appalled as he told me that he's very careful about his indiscretions. So careful in fact, he needs to see a medical report to make sure his would-be-mistress has no sexually transmitted infections. And then, as if it were in slow motion, in a very serious tone, he said, "I'm very oral..."

Just sit with this for a moment.

"I'm very oral..."

Imagine yourself in this same situation. I am betting that if you're a woman, you have been in this kind of predicament at least once.

"I'm very oral..."

Okay—proceed.

He explained that there was no way he was going to contract a sexual disease and bring it home to his wife. He added that he would literally want to kill someone who gave him an STD. KILL! Whoa!!!!! There I was in my cute skirt and dangly earrings trying to write an order. I can't remember exactly what I said, but I found a graceful way to change the subject, took my order and left. I'll admit, I didn't feel as if he demeaned me. I thought he was acting like a lunatic and I chose to say nothing, other than make fun of him with my friends at a later date. He didn't hurt or scare me. I was safe. He just showed me that men can be pigs and sometimes, they almost can't help themselves from behaving like Neanderthals. Sometimes. Some men. Not all the time and not all men. **This is why we need enforcement of sexual harassment laws.** Perhaps if those laws were enforced (because women can be guilty as well) people wouldn't feel so comfortable doing it.

I could have made a complaint and gotten this man in big trouble. Maybe if I had complained, no one would have cared. The point is he should NEVER have addressed me this way in a work situation. He did because he felt there would be no consequences for him. Men are sexual and they view sex differently than women. In this particular instance, I will say, "Boys will be boys." It doesn't excuse anything. It doesn't mean men can be pigs and we should all accept it. To me, it means that when men are only interested in sex, they should understand when to shut the fuck up about it in a business setting. This means we need rules and laws. This is another great reason to VOTE for people who will work to make these laws enforceable and create laws that we currently lack.

Does all of this mean I hate men? No. OF COURSE NOT! Just had to throw that out there. And aside from the "oral" comment, he was a pleasant customer.

Another example of a male customer who acted like a pig was "Ron," a state employee. He was harmless but a total pig. I would visit him, we'd chat and he would take forever to place his order because his dungeon of an office didn't see much excitement, so when a female sales representative wanted him to spend money, he kept her there as long as he could. Hey, can you blame him? I would probably do the same if a cute dude visited my office. When I would hurry him along, he would always tell me that if I wore a white tank top with no bra, his orders would be bigger. (Insert sarcastic eye roll.) I would tell him he was a pig and to "dream on" and we'd laugh. He would always order from me and even help me with referrals. His juvenile comments never bothered me. I wasn't bothered for a few reasons: I knew that he knew I would never wear a tank top with no bra for him. EVER. I also accepted the fact that I was in a male-dominated industry and this is just how it is. Sometimes men say stupid shit. My mother told me more than once to report him, but I argued that he didn't touch me and he didn't ever imply that the only way he would order was by me doing him a "favor." This was how I saw it: I would have lost half of my customer base every time a man said something sexist and I reported it. Not to mention, I would be filing reports on a daily basis. I chose not to get upset over the little stuff. I told them they were pigs in an effort to show them they were not going to get away with anything more and I did my best to keep it light. Here's the rub: If I were in that position now—as an activist for women—I can only guess I would still choose not to report these men because I would lose them as customers. I would lose money and possibly, my job. No one wants a "drama queen" or a "troublemaker" working for them, and the boy's club still has enough power to squash a woman who dares to stand up for herself. I've experienced that first hand. I did speak up for myself in other work situations and in one instance, I lost the account. This is why we need LAWS that are enforced!

When I was younger, I found it much more difficult to speak up for myself when men said inappropriate things to me. The hardest thing for me to deal with was/is when a man just dismisses me. It's very a difficult situation. If you stay silent, you give them your power and allow for them to have the control they are seeking. If you speak up, you're called "hysterical" or "emotional" or the "angry feminist." As I age, I have been able to find that fine-line of speaking up in a way that gets the point across without being accused of being the unhinged female who can't handle difficult situations, but some will still go there no matter what. And trust me, if a woman stands up to certain men, they will say she is hysterical, because male bullies don't like to be called out, especially by a woman.

In my early twenties I had an enormous crush on a gorgeous Swede. I might as well have been a big bowl of mush with no brain. I liked him too much, and that resulted in me giving away all of my power. He literally told me his life was more important than mine because he managed a rock band and I worked at a department store. Can you imagine?? How ridiculous. He wasn't *trying* to be a jerk. That's just the way he saw it. I didn't know how to respond to him, so I didn't. But I never forgot how it made me feel. If he said that to me now, I would laugh in his face and tell him some things he probably wouldn't like. I didn't do that when I was younger because he was a babe and I wanted him to like me—so much so that I sold myself short. I KNOW there are women out there who will do this, no matter their age or social status. I really wish they would stop. But I can't be worried about them and neither should you. Worry about yourself and realize that any man who needs to make himself seem more important than you FOR ANY REASON will eventually lose his allure and one day, when you look at him, you'll just feel disgust. But I do know the power of sexual attraction. Sigh.

The last example I'll provide comes from a wealthy man I used to date. A macho buffoon. He said so many ridiculous things to me but two stick out. The first is when we were dating. I was living alone in a small apartment. I was paying my own bills and working two jobs. I wasn't hurting for money, but I wasn't rolling in dough either. I never asked him or anyone for help and took pride in the fact I was independent. I'm not sure how it came up, but one evening while in my living room, he said to me, "You have less money than the homeless man at the 7-11."

Yes, he said that. I told you he was a buffoon. The fact that what he said wasn't true made no difference to me. He insulted me. He was suggesting that my home was less than par and he humiliated me. I never cried or allowed it to get in the way of how I lived my life, but I always remembered it and how it made me feel. Without realizing it, he was attempting to make me feel less than he was. He had a need to point out that he was superior. Why? I'm not sure. Perhaps it gave him a feeling of satisfaction to believe he was better than me because he had a nicer home. I did feel inadequate and I allowed him to do that to me. I was young and I had no idea how to even begin to address what he said at the time. So, I allowed him to make me feel inferior.

I did save the best for last. Eventually, my relationship with the wealthy buffoon ended on decent terms. I was never in love with him—much to his chagrin—and that enabled me to continue to touch base with him from time to time after our dating relationship ended. One afternoon, we were sitting in a coffee house on Ventura Boulevard and catching up with each other's lives. He had since gotten married and was a new, proud father to an adorable baby girl. The patrons were predominantly women and the tables were very close together. I was thirty-seven years old and, once again, I don't remember exactly how the conversation started, but I think he was pointing out how I was single and if I wanted to get married and have children, I'd better hurry up. And that's when he said the stupidest thing any man has ever said to me: "Women over forty lose their value."

I sat there dumbfounded, not at all upset, as I'd grown used to his buffoonery, but the fact that he had the audacity to say this particular gem left me speechless—and that's RARE! As I gathered my thoughts, I quickly assessed the situation and looked around the room at all the other women in close proximity. I spoke in a loud enough voice so that I would be heard. I repeated what he said, and as I expected, all the women stopped what they were doing and glared at him. He immediately put his hands in the air and said, "I don't make the rules." I laughed at him. I told him he was a buffoon.

When I turned forty, I sent him an email letting him know that I had started losing value—just to mess with him. His words didn't hurt me. I had enough confidence at that point in my life to see he is just a confused man. I am infuriated that too many people, including women, buy into the idea that a mature woman is worthless. This perception is more pronounced in American culture because our media tells us so. And we buy into it.

It's not always easy to stand up for yourself when you're a young woman. It's not always easy when you're older either. Sometimes youth prevents us from having the confidence to say what needs to be said. Sometimes, our paychecks depend on us having to pick our battles and let certain things go because we know we won't win. Before you give up hope and think there is nothing you can do, please consider what you *can* do. It took me a while to feel as if I could stand up for myself. I have always been outspoken but I haven't always stood up. Age helps. After a while, you realize that it's more important to be true to yourself, although not every woman/person gets to that point.

There's not much we can do about what comes out of the mouths of buffoons, but we *can* do something about policies that govern other aspects of our lives. The most important thing you can do is to vote for the politicians who will make sure policies and rules are in place to keep the workplace fair and free of harassment and discrimination. **This is key.** Legislation is the start and eventually will change societal views. It never, ever happens overnight.

The Cosby Show is a great example of how society slowly accepts ideas that were once rejected. First, there was legislation. Black people were freed from slavery. Then, they won the right to vote (which should have been a birthright) and eventually, the civil rights movement helped with race discrimination. Obviously, we aren't cured of racism, but we have come a long way and *The Cosby Show* helped to change society's perception. Americans fell in love with the Huxtables. They were an affluent African-American family with a working father *and* mother as strong role models. Cliff and Clair Huxtable commanded respect. The show broke molds and helped Americans become more tolerant. Fortunately, not every American needed this lesson. But the idea is that as children, when we see something in pop culture, we accept it and it helps to form our worldview.

My grandfather was attacked by a group of young black men and was unable to get beyond that scary memory. He never completely accepted black people as equal. I argued with him about this many times. I failed to help him see his prejudice was a waste of energy. His children do not share his views. They grew up in a more progressive culture and their children (me, my siblings and cousins) have no issue with people of color. In short, perceptions are changed with generations and usually don't happen immediately.

As for things men say to chip away at women's confidence, the only advice I can offer is do not allow anyone, man or woman, to make you feel poorly about who you are or what you have. It may sound trite but it is true. There are so many people who need to berate someone else in order to make themselves feel superior, and in those cases it always stems from their own insecurity and has nothing to do with their target. It's best to pity them, hope and wish them the best, and allow yourself to be free from their negativity.

And I'll say it again and again and again—**vote in every election** for the candidates who will work for equality. Progressive women are the best bet for gender equality because women have experienced gender inequality. That is the most powerful way women can make a difference.

Your Pretty Little Head

You shouldn't only post about all the egregious things happening to women.
You need to get out more.
You have issues with your father and only talk about your mother.
Feminism is killing you.
You know that you have enough rights, why must you take on the ERA?
You must hate men.
You should only focus on the positive.

These are some of the nuggets I've heard from men who identify as progressives. Sometimes they email me or sometimes they say it to my face. Most feel comfortable emailing me because they only know me from social media. They read my Facebook and blog posts and make all kinds of assumptions about me. The worst was when an angry man, who has been insulting and has made personal attacks on my Facebook friends, told me I have deep anger issues with my father. He sent me a private email to ~~explain~~ mansplain what he thought my problem was. I attempted to be civil and made him aware that he didn't know what he was talking about, and that my family was none of his concern. He continued to enlighten me on my own life and I defriended him. Another social media casualty.

Ever since I've been vocal about women's rights, and especially the Equal Rights Amendment, I have noticed that certain men are not happy about it. They come at me with what appears to be concern for my well-being. They attempt to guide me in the right direction—which, to them, is for me to shut up about it. My posts make them *"wince,"* as I have been told.

What they fail to realize is they only add fuel to my fire. For all the talk about how unattractive angry feminists are, they are actually creating not only an angry feminist but a more determined one. With every little dig and every little suggestion, I only grow firmer in my resolve.

It is at this point that I would like to point out that there are MANY men I know, including my father, who are for women's rights and believe the ERA should be fully ratified. I have learned much from the men I have met in my journey as a feminist/activist, as well as men I have known my whole life. There are many who get it. Yet there are still too many who feel uncomfortable with the notion that women should have as much power as they do. "Might makes right." My mother recently said these words to me. The idea behind it is that a man is physically stronger than a woman and because of this, she must obey or face possible violence. Yes, this is a *major* generalization. No, every man doesn't feel this way. But it does ring true on many levels. I see it every day. I have been told by progressive men that I shouldn't go on a "witch hunt" when I express desire to single out male senators who are not supporting gender equality. Witch hunt???? Whaaaaatttttt???? A man actually said this to me. A friend. A man who identifies as a feminist.

These little things men say to women add up. After years and years of little digs, anger builds up and then we literally become The Angry Feminists—as if showing emotion is a bad thing. Last I heard, showing emotion was human and a good way to move past the problem.

Feminist: The Other "F" Word

"Feminism is a socialist, anti-family political movement that encourages women to leave their husbands, kill their children, practice witchcraft, destroy capitalism and become lesbians." **Pat Robertson, U.S. televangelist.**

"Feminist ideology teaches that it is demeaning to women to care for their babies, and therefore the role of motherhood should be eliminated...so that women can fulfill themselves in the paid labor force." **Anti-feminist Phyllis Schlafly**

"In a nutshell, women are angry. They're also defensive, though often unknowingly. That's because they've been raised to think of men as the enemy. Armed with this new attitude, women pushed men off their pedestal (women had their own pedestal, but feminists convinced them otherwise) and climbed up to take what they were taught to believe was rightfully theirs. Now the men have nowhere to go." **Anti-feminist Suzanne Venker, *The War On Men*. FOX News online.**

"I think all real females are right-wingers, and I can tell you that based on experience—and my bodyguard will back me up on this—all pretty girls are right-wingers."

"If we took away women's right to vote, we'd never have to worry about another Democrat president. It's kind of a pipe dream, it's a personal fantasy of mine, but I don't think it's going to happen. And it is a good way of making the point that women are voting so stupidly, at least single women." **Ann Coulter**

"I prefer to call the most obnoxious feminists what they really are: feminazis." **Rush Limbaugh**

***

What comes to your mind when you hear the term feminist? Is it positive or negative? Does it bring to mind a modern-day woman, or do you visualize images from the 1970s women's liberation movement?

Feminism is often associated with a liberal ideology, but it isn't limited to liberals. When you break it down, you see that it's about equality in the eyes of the law. Why has it become a partisan issue? It really isn't one. It isn't a Democratic cause. It is a HUMAN RIGHTS ISSUE.

For the most part, the new feminist movement is growing and evolving, but according to the right, it is falsely presented as a liberal tactic to provide women with free birth control. Why is this? Why can't women on both sides of the aisle come together in the name of sisterhood? Even liberal feminists divide themselves by criticizing each other for not being stronger or better feminists. It has become such a divisive term, even though the root and the motivation has always been about equality and individual power.

As I mentioned previously, a common, veiled attempt to degrade the meaning is to claim "I'm a humanist," as opposed to being a feminist. This just irritates me to no end. While there is nothing wrong with wanting equality for everyone, this implies that feminism is a negative way to be. Feminists ARE humanists. Isn't it interesting but incredibly depressing that feminism is blamed for the downfall of American values, and the Equal Rights Amendment is currently in time-out with an expired deadline? The two terms that translate to equality for women have been soiled by those who wish to keep women from real freedom. I have received numerous emails and comments from men who identify as liberal, who in an effort to correct me, tell me the proper term is really humanist. They'll say it like this, "Awww Kim, come on now..." When I am confronted this way, I feel set up to be that "hysterical feminist" because they know they are being patronizing. Of course a profanity bomb goes off in my head and my gut instinct is to start verbally abusing these people. Who they hell are you to take that tone with me? "Aww come on now..." ??? As if I am unable to see how it *really* is. But I keep my cool and argue the facts. The facts are simple. Women are not yet equal.

A man asked me if the reason I became a feminist was because of a negative event in my life. In other words, he wanted to know if the reason I fight for women's rights has to do with something horrible that happened to me. He assumed that is what it took. The answer is quite simple. I was raised by a feminist—my mother is a strong woman who believes in fairness and equality. I didn't become one because of men. I became an activist after Rush Limbaugh called Sandra Fluke a slut. I have always been a feminist.

Maybe you are one of those people who think feminists are nasty harpies. Maybe you have friends who don't want to be identified as feminists. I have heard from some young girls that they have friends who tell them they are for women's rights but they are not feminists. My question is why? What is the reason? What have they heard? Why are they criticizing an entire movement that has secured the right to vote for women? A movement that has fought against gender discrimination and has made sure that property is passed down to daughters and not just sons? If you or your friends believe feminism is a bad thing, you may have been influenced by people who don't understand what feminism is and/or people who don't want to see women on an equal footing with their male counterparts.

There are people, women as well as men, who don't want women to have power. These people seek to co-opt feminist terminology in an effort to discredit feminism as a movement. This has made the recent rollbacks in women's rights possible. Apathy and ignorance has allowed it to happen. Money talks. The ability to shape the conversation depends on having the money to control the message.

What is the message? It's the argument that feminism is a dirty word and should be replaced. It is a series of denying or taking away rights. I ran across a great meme on Facebook that describes it perfectly. There was no name, so I can't say who came up with it, but whoever it was, I applaud you and I added a couple of points of my own.

–Gender pay inequality, i.e. paying women less and denying women the ability to have higher paying positions or positions of power and authority.

– Restricting or outlawing abortion.

– Restricting or denying women the right to birth control.
– Restricting or ignoring women's place in history by not including it in school curriculums.
– Blaming women who are raped.
– Accusing victims of rape of lying about it.
– Making it more difficult for women to vote.
– Restricting or denying affordable healthcare for women and children.
– Blaming women for ruining the traditional family dynamic.
– Painting sexist men as victims of a feminized culture.
– Using epithets to describe women who fight for equality. Feminazi. Slut. Bitch. Whore. Cunt.

Here's what really concerns me: Many young women have decided that feminists are a negative group. They assume we are the unpleasant stereotype that opponents of feminism say we are. Too many young women also assume that American women have complete and total equality and nothing left to fight for; that the fight is over and we won.

Nope. We still have mountains to climb and feminism will continue to evolve to fight the battles not yet won.

Opponents of feminism often portray feminists as destructive, humorless harpies who hate men and only focus on our vaginas. They say feminists have ruined the American family and the sanctity of marriage. We are not allowed to proclaim there might be something unfair or not altogether true about the teachings of Christianity. It's a social no-no. We have to leave religion alone. But Christianity puts the woman below the man. If this is what you believe, you probably wouldn't be reading this book. If you believe a woman is less than a man, I honestly don't know what to say to you—other than I think you are wrong.

When women are earning 77¢ on the dollar compared to their male counterparts,[1] it also means that women will be collecting less Social Security in retirement. Until it becomes illegal in every state for pharmacists to deny women birth control legally prescribed by their doctors, women need to rise up and fight the patriarchy and the subjugation that still exists in America today.

Women may feel equal in the United States, but it isn't yet guaranteed in the Constitution. We have witnessed that it is quite easy to overturn or repeal a law. If you live in a state where women have a protection against pay discrimination, all it takes is one legislator to change things up. Constitutional amendments are not easy to change and they provide blanket protection for people in every state.

I am a feminist. **I do not hate men**. I was never accused of hating men before I became an activist. However, since I have become an outspoken advocate for women's rights, I am accused of hating men often—as are many women who just want to see gender equality. I don't criticize women if they choose to be housewives because to me, it is all about choice. No one should ever be forced to live in a way that has been dictated by anyone else. EVER!

Feminism is about **equality**. It's the declaration that women are equal in the eyes of the law and their equality needs to be codified in our Constitution. Take the time to familiarize yourself with the more than two thousand pieces of anti-women, restrictive, reproductive legislation that has been introduced or passed by Republicans since 2011 and ask yourself: "Am I a feminist?" Do you believe women should have the ability to terminate a pregnancy? Should women be treated the same as men under the law? Should a woman earn as much as a man does for doing the same work? If you answered yes to all, you are a feminist!

The '80s proved to be a decade of progress for women, but it didn't come without its problems. We saw women executives earning impressive salaries, new laws protecting women from sexual harassment and the term "Superwoman" emerged. Young women felt empowered and thought the fight for equality was over. It isn't. We haven't completely arrived—yet.

One of the problems that emerged from the '70s feminist movement was the idea that women can have it all. This left many women very confused. Think about it. Women were told they could get married, have children AND be CEOs. Men? Well, they just kept on with no real role change. This meant it was all left up to women. It does work for *some* women. My

Republican girlfriend is married with kids and earns more than her husband. She was back to work as soon as a few weeks after giving birth and this was her choice. It wouldn't be mine. If I were to get married and have children, I would want the option to stay at home as long as I wanted to. I would eventually want to work, but for at least two or three years, I would want to be a stay-at-home mom. That would be *my* choice.

While it is easy to find fault with the feminist movement and blame the people who fought hard for workplace equality for the confusing messaging of the Superwoman ideal, we must remember, they were venturing into uncharted territory and they didn't realize how things would play out. Their main goal was to guarantee that women HAVE CHOICES. These are the issues that weren't addressed in detail several decades ago and that led to confusion and disappointment.

Don't dismiss what was accomplished. Don't allow the rights and freedoms that were fought for with blood, sweat and tears—LITERALLY—by women who came before you, to be taken away because you can't be bothered with expanding your mind, or you want to believe "feminist" means a hippie chick who doesn't shave or women who insist that all feminists subscribe to exactly the same ideology.

Women need to find solidarity and leave behind the notion that being a strong, competent, outspoken woman is negative. We must embrace the idea that feminists come in all shapes, sizes, backgrounds and political ideologies. We have work to do and unless we band together, we will continue to struggle to keep the rights that were fought for and won by the women and *men* before us.

It's the 21st century. What's the hold up? Seriously! Women make up half of the population. We give birth to the entire human race. We deserve a constitutional guarantee.

Feminism And Social Media

I presently run the Rock The Slut Vote Facebook page. I make no money doing this. The one thing it provides for me is a voice. Not *my* voice, but a voice for women. I have learned the hard way that when I post my opinion with an article or meme, I am occasionally scolded by some (NOT ALL) fans. So it goes something like this: I post something. For whatever reason, some fans (NOT ALL—not even most) of the page don't like it. They comment and then let me know they will unlike the page. "I AM UNLIKING YOUR PAGE!!!!!!!!!!!!!!!!!" Or "I used to like this page but your post is propaganda and you can't be bothered to fact check." When I see this happening and if it offends enough people, I will take the post down. I then post what has transpired and note that I removed the content. People then criticize me for being censored. Of course, it's not everyone on the page who does this. Am I clear about this? IT IS NOT EVERYONE, but I have seen it happen time and again on RTSV and other feminist pages. The goal of RTSV is to keep women and men informed and up to date with all the current legislation attacking women's rights. It is also a platform to discuss women's issues and share ideas and solutions. In fact, I have learned A LOT by reading the comments. This can be said of all the pages I oversee. I am not always able to read every comment, but I count on people to help broaden my thinking. My mind has been changed when people present fact-based arguments. If someone makes a comment with no link to back up what they say, I do an online search. I learn all kinds of things by staying open to other people's opinions and ideas and to facts that I may be unaware of. Thank you to all who have helped me learn.

RTSV grows daily and this tells me there is a need for it. I do my best to make sure the latest headlines are up so that we are armed with knowledge, especially during election seasons. I don't maintain the page to stroke my ego. It's work. And if I wish for the page to grow and for fans to get updates, I must post every single day. I NEVER get a day off, EVER, not even holidays. It's just the way Facebook algorithms work. If you don't post consistently, you lose your reach. Thankfully, Facebook has a feature that allows page admins to schedule posts in advance, otherwise, I'd be chained to my computer.

I get that everyone has an opinion and I am always open to suggestions. I may not always take them, but I AM open. I have taken and applied suggestions, but to get your knickers in a twist over a meme (a picture with a message) and leave a page, any page that helps to inform, for something so insignificant as a typo is juvenile. I can only speak for myself. If I am made aware that something I've posted is inaccurate, I will address it. I usually remove it and create a status update with the correct information. I am not perfect. I am human and make mistakes. Do you stop watching the news because they made a typo in a graphic?

MSNBC has a tendency to beat a lot of dead horses. They go on and on and on sometimes about an issue that a show host might be very interested in, but the audience might like to see some of the other stories that are happening. I still enjoy watching that network and I don't call the 800 number and scream that I don't like the network. And if I do decide that I don't want to watch MSNBC any more, I will just do so without making a big deal.

Social media makes it very easy to have a knee-jerk reaction. I know because it's happened to me. I learned that it is better to think before I type an angry response to something. There was an instance where I saw that a man I didn't know commented on a friend's post—something that made me extremely angry. I actually practiced self-control and didn't comment. I told myself to ignore it, but I was unable to let it go and I went back to it. I read it again and I think actual smoke came out of my ears, and this time I made the STUPID decision to reply while I was angry. His commentary had something to do with Sarah Palin and how she used crosshairs over politicians' faces as targets. Rather than really considering an intelligent or well thought out reply, I was REALLY sarcastic and I asked if he would send pictures of his family to me so that I could put them on my website with crosshairs over their faces. I thought it was rather obvious that I wasn't being serious. If I was serious, I wouldn't have asked him to voluntarily send pictures of his family to me. He didn't, or he didn't want to, understand that I was using sarcasm because he also reacted in an emotional way and it quickly escalated. He was angry. I was angry. We BOTH called the FBI on each other—BECAUSE OF A FACEBOOK POST that went south. How STUPID is that? I think it's pretty fucking stupid.

Do I blame him? No. I was the main idiot. His comment was not on my page. It had NOTHING to do with me. Instead of ignoring it, or making an effort to have a rational dialogue, I immediately went for the jugular and I was insulting as well. He chose to believe that I was threatening his family. Interestingly enough, in the end, we wound up chatting in an email—this is how I found out he called the FBI on me—and we laughed it off and ended on good terms. But seriously, there is a lesson here. I learned it. I learned that sometimes you see things online that piss you off, and it's always best to take a few breaths before you decide to get all crazy about it and stir up other peoples' anger. Since we are unable to hear the inflection in a written post, I have found it's best to ask what a person means. Sometimes someone is trying to make a joke but the attempt is misunderstood. What they think is silly might sound really awful to someone else. All it takes is asking for clarification and not assuming something and immediately going for an angry response.

My FBI story is a perfect way to illustrate that, as a country, we are divided. People are scared. I don't agree with every opinion out there, but I seriously do my best to overlook the smaller stuff so that I can focus on what is truly important. A meme is JUST A MEME. It is not a definition of an entire ideology. When I see people so angry and so quick to judge those who are ON THEIR SIDE, I get very worried and wonder if we'll ever be able to come together as a whole, despite our individual differences, and effect REAL CHANGE.

Feminism is both political and social. The political side is cut and dried. Equality in the eyes of the law. Let's focus on and pass the Equal Rights Amendment. Let's see real equality for the sexes and then we can nitpick and argue over the social aspects of feminism. Equality *should be* the easy part.

***

I can post a good meme that makes everyone happy, or I can post an outrageous article where some asshole politician says something completely ignorant about women and those posts get a lot of shares, comments and likes. I post about the ERA and it's freaking crickets. **CRICKETS**!!! Sure, there are the die-hard activists who will share, but most ignore it. I don't understand this. Don't you want constitutional protection? Why do silly memes get thousands of shares but ERA posts get ignored? Kim Kardashian's Facebook page has millions of followers. More people care more about her tweets and posts than about their own equality.

I also see feminists argue amongst themselves about things that are very nitpicky. It is such a monumental of waste of time. It doesn't mean that your individual opinion is not valid or important, but what it does mean is that when we allow ourselves to get wrapped up in the arguments and the idea that one person is a better feminist than the other, WE ALL LOSE. It is, in part, why we are still struggling. Back in the 1970s, women were very angry about inequality and they were loud. They had little or no opportunity to make it on their own. Their loud voices helped to create a more equal footing, but some also did themselves a disservice. By criticizing women who really enjoyed being stay-at-home-moms and using shame, they turned many women off to the idea of feminism. When someone is introduced to a new idea by being shamed, it stands to reason they won't want to learn more or be a part of it. It's all in the presentation. Take these two examples. Which one would you be more open to?

— You are crazy for wanting to be a stay-at-home mom. You are just a Stepford wife who makes sammiches for your controlling husband. YOU are a disgrace and an embarrassment. Go ask your hubby for permission to iron his shirt and wash his underwear! Maybe he'll give you a few bucks to go grocery shopping.

— Have you ever considered there is more to life than being a stay-at-home-mom? Wouldn't it be great if women were able to use their college educations to go into the work force and earn an equal paycheck and help support their families? If something happened to your husband, wouldn't you like to know that you could handle your family's finances if you had to? And what if, God forbid, you want to leave your marriage? Wouldn't it be nice to know that you can take care of yourself and not *have* to depend on a man?

Phyllis Schlafly used a soft sell approach to stop the

ratification of the ERA. She told women to dress like ladies and smile when they delivered their message of "conservative values." Like it or not, it works. Her messaging was nice and more appealing to the women who were on the fence, than that from the women who used anger to make their point. There was, and still is, a whole generation of women who need to feel comfortable with being feminists. What they don't need is to be yelled at by a bunch of angry women telling them they are horrible people because they depend on their husbands or are not on the front lines of the movement. Some women don't want to work. And that's okay. Keep in mind also, women like Schlafly's followers never knew any other way of life. Their roles were pretty much defined by the times they lived in. It's like being born poor and that is all one knows. And then someone comes along and yells at them because they are poor. If a woman wants to stay home, take care of the kids and make cupcakes, that is HER choice and no one has the right to tell her she is wrong for wanting that kind of life. People should always be able to **choose** how they live their own lives.

Isn't it more important to find ways to further progress by working together on the big stuff? Isn't it more important to be tolerant and accept that everyone will not make the same choices you do? You can still have an opinion, but to demand, insist or push your agenda on another is exactly what feminists are fighting against.

I'll make a comparison with religion and because it was within my sphere as I grew up, I will cite Christianity. My maternal grandmother was a practicing Catholic. She attended church every Sunday. It was her faith. She practiced it quietly. Maybe she believed I was on the way to hell but if she did, she never said anything. She was a beautiful soul and an amazing woman. She accepted that people hold different beliefs and she didn't feel the need to convert them. I wasn't brought up in a religious home. But I realize there are a lot of Christians out there. My opinion of Christianity is not relevant or important. I do have a real problem with anyone who tries to make me live by Christian standards. I never force my spiritual beliefs on anyone. So, if someone wishes to practice Christianity, that's great. Just leave me out of it. The only people who know what and how I believe are people who ask me and even then, I present it in a way that lets them know it is *my* belief. I am not trying to pull them over to my way of thinking. In fact, I enjoy talking with someone who feels differently than I do, and we can have a civil conversation about it. It's rare, but when it happens, it's awesome.

My goal, especially when it pertains to Rock The Slut Vote, is not to try to make anyone like me. I am not looking for, nor am I asking for, sympathy or praise. I just want people to rally together for the greater good. I get very worried when I see groups of people who want the same thing halting progress because they are weighed down with arguments over how to achieve the end goal.

My wish is that no matter how much of a feminist you are, that you allow for different ways of seeing the issues and find ways to work together toward equality. When you are having a conversation or are on a social media page, THINK before you react. Don't assume—unless it's a troll who is obviously looking to elicit an emotional response. Ask what people mean before you reply in anger. Trust me on this. People will call the FBI on you!

Feminism is a good thing. It is not exclusionary; people can be, but the movement isn't. It is one aspect of human equality, a sub-category like LGBT rights or racial and voting rights.

There are all kinds of people, men and women, who are working very hard so that all women will achieve full equality. People you don't know and will most likely never meet are tirelessly working for **your** rights. They attend judiciary committee meetings. They make phone calls to politicians. They call voters and urge them to be informed. They protest and picket. They donate money to causes that further education. Sometimes they risk their lives and their freedoms, and they do it for you and your children. Please don't discount their actions and dismiss the term feminism because someone gave you a false idea about what it really means. Don't ignore the women who went to jail so that you could vote. What if you fought hard and gave up a big chunk of your life, only to be ignored or slapped in the face by a new generation who can't be bothered to pay attention? If you want to follow Kim Kardashian, by all means do so, but don't allow the glitz to distract you from what is really important—what will be important for the women of your daughter's generation.

UPDATE

It is April 22, 2014. As I edit this book and get it ready for release, I would like to report a very encouraging sign.

In this chapter I wrote about how the ERA is not exciting to people on social media. Things are changing. Both President Jimmy Carter and Hillary Clinton have recently voiced the desire to see it ratified. I am noticing that people are now starting to pay attention. This month, Supreme Court Justice Ruth Bader Ginsburg spoke out in favor of the ERA. I posted the article on many large pages on Facebook and it was widely shared. On my wall alone it got over 165 shares. I feel incredibly hopeful and more confident that we will get this DONE!

***

Young women/people seem to be under the impression that the fight for equality is over. This is dangerous because it makes the accomplishments we *have* made more vulnerable. How, you ask? Apathy, that is how.

There are two things that have taken on a negative meaning by too many: Feminism and the Equal Rights Amendment. Why, just today, I was accused of being a man-hater. AGAIN. An Internet troll by the name of Doug, commented on a meme I posted. The meme was a quote from my book, *The Virgin Diaries*. It read; "My parents made it clear that we were not supposed to have sex until married, and if we did, we were sluts. Men have sex with whores, but marry virgins. ~ Female. 34. I was 16 when I lost my virginity." Here's what Doug had to say, "Kim is a charter member of the man haters club. Hey Kim, do me a favor and do not paint me with that broad brush you carry."

What the ever-loving fuck?! Talk about a broad brush! After many comments on the thread, it was clear that Doug assumed the quote was mine and that it is the way I view all men. When many of us tried to explain that he misunderstood the meme, he went missing. His accusation is an all too common assumption about feminism that just won't die. Feminists don't hate men. Jeez—the only people who perpetuate that stupidity are the people who are intimidated by women who aren't afraid to speak up and be strong.

My male friend, whom I will call "Rob," vehemently believes women should have equality. He doesn't understand why more women aren't demanding it. Rob is in his 50s, so it came as quite a shock to me when he said (and I am paraphrasing) "After women gained some equality, the thing that happened was, they just started cussing and became openly crude. I have never understood that. Rather than men cleaning it up, we are just **all** vulgar now." Sigh. And fuck. I immediately explained that, because he is my dear friend and I know where his heart is, I will not jump to anger. I told him that is one of the most sexist things anyone can ever say about feminism and I calmly explained why.

Being a feminist isn't a magic license to use profanity. Women have ***always*** used profanity. The difference is they didn't always feel comfortable using profanity in public or around men. It was a social no-no and not ladylike. In some cases women who dared to swear risked violence or public humiliation. What a fucking drag for them! And as far as being crude—some human beings enjoy a certain amount of crude humor. I am one of those humans. It has nothing to do with equality in the eyes of the law. But it does mean we live in a society that allows—oh how I despise that word—women to do or say whatever they want as long as it's legal. It isn't up to any one person to give another person permission to swear or be crude, and the very fact that there are those who try to control women and "keep them in their pretty little place" just means they have insecurity problems. As far as I'm concerned, they can just fuck right off.

The way I see it, the most important aspect of feminism is political: gender equality in the eyes of the law. It means if I am doing the same job as a man with the same qualifications and a similar resumé, I expect to be paid the same. If I find that a man is earning more for the same job description, I should have the right to sue the company if they refuse to pay me the same wages. It means that as a woman, I have the same rights and opportunities as men. Period. As America evolves and feminism is more accepted, the social aspect will bleed into our personal lives. Just because a woman uses the term "shit" doesn't mean that feminism has opened the door to a vulgar society. What it *does* mean is men and women who are simply used to, and have accepted, the patriarchal way will slowly adapt to equality and eventually, it won't even be an issue.

What's really awful is that the negativity associated with the word feminism is spreading to the liberal community, and prominent role models are distancing themselves from the word. Susan Sarandon, who is an activist and amazing actress, was interviewed by The Guardian[2] in June of 2013 and had this to say: "I think of myself as a humanist because I think it's less alienating to people who think of feminism as being a load of strident bitches and because you want everyone to have equal pay, equal rights, education and healthcare. It's a bit of an old-fashioned word. It's used more in a way to minimize you. My daughter, who is 28, doesn't even relate to the word 'feminist' and she is definitely in control of her decisions and her body."

The following month, Jaime Franchi penned a rebuttal titled *An Open Letter to Susan Sarandon on Feminism*[3] in a blog, *The Broadside*. Jaime wrote in part:

"If the word 'feminist' has negative connotations, running away from the word won't fix that. Whatever new word you come up with will eventually take on the same negative connotations. Because the problem isn't with feminists; it's with those who demonize feminism. Sometime we like to complain about how the word 'feminism' has become associated with negative stereotypes; well that's been true since the beginning. Look at any literature or political cartoons or propaganda from anti-suffragists, for example—you'll see many of the same stereotypes you do today. It wasn't because those women called themselves feminists; they were attacked for what they fought for, not for what they called themselves. It's the same today. Does the term 'humanist' as you suggested, cover the ground we want addressed in a more palatable terminology?

'Humanism' is *not* feminism-for-everyone. It is a separate, long-established philosophy of doing good in the world without religious incentives. But humanism is about valuing the individual and individual rights over societal rights. Feminism is about working together to make the world a better place for myself *and others.* I am so sorry to read this. We need to stand together and show the world how amazingly great feminists are—not retreat from the word because we fear someone will think us bitchy."

I couldn't have said it better myself. Jaime summed it up perfectly. I highly recommend looking up the blog post online. She has a lot more to say and it's all really important when understanding what feminists have accomplished.

It boils down to semantics. It doesn't seem Susan has a problem with feminism, but she has allowed those who wish to demonize the word to dictate how she identifies herself, and I think that is really sad. I love Susan Sarandon, always have and always will, and if I ever have the opportunity to have a cup of coffee with her, I would love to address this with her. I would also tell her that by distancing herself from the word, she is disrespecting the feminists who paved the way for her equality and her ability to have the platform she enjoys. I know, I'm dreaming.

One might argue that American women already have equality and there is no need to secure it. In fact, many do argue this. To that, all I have to do is point out that a current law can be overturned. Let's take a look at discrimination laws. It would seem that if a legislator wanted to strip the rights of women away, they might not get away with creating a bill that does this in a blatant way. BUT they can achieve this with riders, which is slipping one bill in with another bill. Here is an example: A Democratic politician in Kentucky writes a bill that says the minimum wage must be raised by one dollar. This bill will get resistance. A Republican may say, "The only way I will vote for this bill is if you add my rider, that if a woman is discriminated against in the workplace, she will not be able to sue her employer." Now, the bill the public hears about is raising the minimum wage and that sounds great! But in order to get that passed, the discriminatory compromise also gets passed. Most voters don't keep up with all the riders attached to the bills. The ERA would make it impossible for this type of hidden legislation to happen because gender discrimination would be against federal law and would trump state laws.

Why are the two BIG issues that represent gender equality, feminism and the Equal Rights Amendment, treated as ugly or negative?

Wake up people. The only folks who will lose when the ERA is passed are the ones who don't want to see women as equal. Too fucking bad. Right? Right!

The Other Kind Of Girl

Lindy West is a blogger for the website *Jezebel*. I bow to her ability to not only succinctly tell a tale but to do so with such fabulousness and intelligence.

West wrote an article titled *Female Purity Is Bullshit* in May of 2013. I read this on a day where my spirits were low. Tears were flowing and I second-guessed myself at every turn. I felt inspired after reading what she wrote and it pulled me out of my self-absorbed funk. She asked if everyone was as annoyed with "purity" as she was. She pointed out the tired and false idea that there are two kinds of women: the good ones who are marriage material and everyone else.

I was immediately reminded of a girl I will call Karen. She was a friend of one of my girlfriends. The three of us went out for a night of fun. Karen was a plain looking girl, a little on the frumpy side, but she was nice and I had a good time hanging out with her. A few days later, my friend told me that Karen said, "We're the kinds of girls men marry. Kimberley is the kind they just want to fuck." As soon as I heard this, I was hurt. I knew why she said it. I have always had a big mouth and appeared confident. I am used to people making false assumptions about me based on my looks. Maybe Karen felt intimidated and threatened by me. She needed to put me down so she could feel better about herself.

When Karen made that comment, I took it to heart. Part of the reason is there is a bit of truth to what she said. I have met many men who were only interested in having sex with me. They see me as a conquest and sex is the prize—not my mind or my heart. Maybe it sounds trite, but good-looking people don't always have easy times because of the way they look. I was so desperate to be accepted and loved that if a man complimented me or phoned me, I really thought he liked *me*. I thought those actions meant I was valuable.

Let me back up here. When I was a teen, boys didn't really like me—or if they did, they didn't admit it. My girlfriends were hooking up with boys, dating and making out and I was the tall girl whom no boy liked. I was pretty but that didn't matter—at least not to me. I was different and you know how kids are. Once, when I was fifteen, I was with a group of teen couples. My best friend suggested that we "turn off the lights and listen to David Bowie." This was code for a group make-out session. I was the only one who had no make-out partner—I hadn't even kissed a boy at that point. The lights went out, the music came on and I sat there HUMILIATED. I snuck out of the room, called my mother and she picked me up. The next time I saw my best friend, she laughed like it was no big deal and said they all wondered what happened to me when they came up for air. I was home, crying because I was different and I felt like no one would ever love me. This was pretty much what it was like for me as a teen. I liked boys. They didn't like me and I watched all of my friends hold hands and go on dates. Just because someone is considered beautiful, it doesn't mean life is a walk in the park. People make wrong assumptions about others all the time.

So, back to Karen's comment having some truth. I was not the popular girl growing up, and when I was in my early twenties my insecurities deepened as I compared myself to the popular actresses and models. Men did ask me out and I did date. But it wasn't all romance and flowers.

My very first boyfriend was a babe. I immediately fell for him. The first time I saw him was when I was a sophomore in high school. He had a girlfriend and I swooned from afar. My junior and senior years were spent at another school. It wasn't until my senior prom that I saw him again. Both of our dates were indisposed and I made my move. I went up to him, said hi and gave him my phone number. I know, I am such a slut! Eventually he called and we went on our first date. It didn't take long before we were an official couple and eventually had sex. He wasn't my first, but I was still relatively new to the world of sexuality. I don't remember exactly how long I waited before going all the way with him, but I will never forget what he told me after we did. He told me that if I had slept with him on our first date, he would never have called me again. His reasoning was that if I had sex with him in a period of time he deemed too soon, he would have assumed I was easy and slutty. I remember feeling so relieved that I didn't sleep with him right away because I liked him soooo much. The truth was I wasn't ready to have sex with him on the first date. I didn't *know* him. It had nothing to do with morality or what anyone else would think. I knew that I needed some time to feel comfortable with him before going all the way. Regardless, I was instantly filled with relief that I had not acted in a slutty way and was able to keep his interest.

What a bunch of bullshit and such a double standard.

Two of my girlfriends married men they slept with on the first date. I am not advocating it or criticizing it; what I am saying is it's ridiculous that men can do this and nobody thinks they are jerks because of it. We hear this all the time. Men get thumbs-up from their buddies for having sex. Women who have and/or enjoy sex are the Whores of Babylon, used goods and not worthy of love. It's the puritanical double standard that ONCE AGAIN gives men the upper hand.

When I was working in a clothing store in the Glendale Galleria in 1989, I met a mall cop. He would stop by the store and flirt with me. He was twenty-six and I was twenty-one. He was a man, not just a "guy" or a "dude." I liked his attention. It made me feel special and mature. He was a nice looking man and eventually, to my delight, he asked me out. I was so excited!!! On the evening of our date, I got all dressed up and I looked very sophisticated in my black skirt and matching jacket. When I saw him approaching the front door through the window, I could see he was wearing shorts and a casual short-sleeved shirt. Disappointed, I hurried and changed so that he didn't think I was as excited as I was. I didn't want to appear too eager or desperate. We went to one of my favorite restaurants on Sunset Boulevard, Mirabelle. It was a nice, adult dinner and afterward we went for a drive in the

Hollywood Hills. He pulled over and we kissed. I sensed something else was happening while we were making out. I opened my eyes and looked down and saw his penis—erect and at attention. He wanted me to handle or suck it or whatever. I was so grossed out and disappointed. I told him no. He really wasn't too concerned about it, and he masturbated in front of me and CLEARLY didn't care what I thought about it. He drove me home. I was confused and I wasn't sure what had just happened. The most HORRIBLE part was that I hoped he still liked me. I cringe sometimes when I look back at how I was so desperate for someone to like me that I chose to view his perverted, inappropriate behavior as acceptable. Keyword: CHOSE. I chose to see things that way. I was a young idiot. When I didn't hear from him, I called him to see if there would be a second date—which made me feel desperate because on some level, I understood that he was an asshole. I just wanted a man I was interested in to like me. He gave me some lame excuse and said he was busy and it ended there. Of course, *now* I am thankful he didn't try again. But at the time, I felt rejected.

Some men see me and all they want is to conquer the six-foot tall blonde with big blue eyes. They don't give a shit about my feelings or who I am as a person. I'm not alone in this. Many women experience only being desired as a body part or as a trophy. The worst part about all of this is that I took it to heart. I didn't have the maturity or life experience to see the difference. Instead of calling these guys assholes and realizing I was better off, I assumed the fault was with me. Somehow I wasn't good enough. I wasn't the coveted female that men wanted to marry. I was the slut whom men just wanted to fuck.

Interestingly, while writing this book—but after I had completed this chapter—a man followed me on Twitter who looked a lot like the perverted man who masturbated in front of me. The name was the same, so I asked him if he ever worked in the Glendale Galleria. He responded that he did. Oh karma, how I LOVE YOU. We communicated back and forth and it was clear he was pretending to forget, or he really did forget acting like an entitled ape on our one and only date so many years ago. He tried to open a sincere dialogue with me and I was evasive. I explained that we had gone out and he was very rude. He laughed it off and pushed for more communication. I finally replied and detailed his actions. I explained what happened and I didn't mince words—and goodness gracious—he just couldn't remember jerking off in front of me. I even told him that I wrote about that experience in my book. He made some comment that suggested that I overreacted or that I am holding on to anger and implied that I might still be carrying a torch for him. Excuse me for having a MEMORY! He didn't even apologize. He ASKED FOR MY PHONE NUMBER. I told him I didn't think it was a very good idea and politely told him to fuck-off. And the irony: he is no longer a mall cop—he advises couples about their love lives.

On another other occasion in my early twenties, I was out to dinner with some folks I had known my whole life. One of the dinner guests, "Jake," brought a date. I had a crush on Jake and he knew it. Jake was also an actor and his date was the daughter of a producer. She was rail thin and had enormous breasts. They were all over each other at dinner and he was bragging about how lucky he was to be with her. I remember feeling a little sad. I couldn't compete with her. My father wasn't a producer and I wasn't rail thin. At some point he announced that there are two kinds of women—there is the kind of woman who men marry and then he looked at me with disdain and said, "and then, there are the **other** kind." I don't believe any of the people at the table were aware of his insult, but I was. It hurt. Once again, I was portrayed to be the kind of woman that men only want to fuck and then discard. I never gave him any indication that I wanted to have sex with him but he *knew* I had a crush on him.

WHY did I allow him to make me feel sad and like I wasn't good enough? It's that fucking purity bullshit! Actually, it's not about purity. It's about people who have terrible self-esteem and their need to take out their own self-hatred on others in the hope they will somehow feel better about themselves.

I am not sharing these personal stories so that you will feel sorry for me. I am a fortunate person. I've had struggles like everyone else. All of my life, people have assumed I've had it easy because of the way I look. I have been lucky and I have been unlucky. No better, no worse.

I fell for the purity bullshit to the degree that I thought I wasn't good enough. I never thought having and enjoying sex made me a slut. It was deeper than that. I believed the messages we hear from commercials and movies and songs and billboards and books and from our peers. The little things people say that chip away at our confidence. I am now in my forties. I look back and it makes me feel so sad that I wasted any time—too much time—thinking I wasn't good enough. I still battle some of those demons, just not to the degree that I did when I was younger.

That sorry old double standard with a heaping serving of sexism says men can have sex and they are studs. Women have to worry about looking like sluts. Don't fall for it. If you have sex, you're not a slut. If you don't have sex, you're not superior. These labels are destructive and they allow for a society where men get to make all the rules. This doesn't mean men should have no power or no say, but they shouldn't get to be the ones dictating morality. They shouldn't be the ones who decide who YOU are. Women need to own their power. Take it. Don't ask for it. If someone doesn't like it, too bad. Don't abuse your power, but don't allow others to take your power from you. We are all EQUAL. Women who like sex are not sluts. We are all just here to learn and love. So stop with the purity bullshit! And thank you, Lindy West, for writing something that took me out of my weepy funk and made me write.

RAPE

Women get blamed when they're raped. Women are told it's their fault because of what they were wearing or that they were a tease or that they had too much to drink. Rape, by definition, is a sexual assault against the victim's will. How then, can anyone be asking for it? And as of late 2013, we've seen states that are forcing women to buy rape insurance![1] RAPE INSURANCE—which is buying separate insurance for abortions—even in the case of rape or incest. This includes rape insurance for young girls—like your daughter. With at least thirty states legally allowing a rapist to sue for visitation and custody rights if the rapist impregnates his victim,[2] women still have a lot of work to do before we can settle into the comfortable idea of equality.

Social media has opened up a new way to discuss and tackle rape. People are talking about it and that's a good thing. There are a lot of opinions and it's a very emotional debate.

Media also plays a very big part of the messaging and unfortunately, it isn't always a helpful message. The victim is blamed. A short skirt, tight pants or a low neckline is an indicator that she was asking for it. Maybe she was drinking and acting like a slut. We've heard it all before and a lot of the time, rape goes unreported because the woman doesn't believe she can win against a system that leans heavily in the rapist's favor. This is not a gender specific problem. Men are very uncomfortable reporting being raped. They would rather not make something like that public, so they suffer in silence to avoid the endless shaming associated with it.

Here are some cold hard statistics:

–Low estimate of the number of women raped every year, according to the Department of Justice: 300,000.[3]

–From the Centers for Disease Control:[4]

 *High estimate of the number of women raped, according to the CDC: 1.3 million.

 *Women who reported being raped in the U.S.: 1 in 5.

 *Men who reported being raped in the U.S.: 1 in 71.

–Percentage of rapes not reported: 54 percent.[5]

–Some female soldiers report not drinking water after 7 p.m. so they don't risk being raped if they use the bathroom.[6]

 In 2013, the Steubenville rape incident became national news. A teenage girl, who was intoxicated and had passed out, was sexually assaulted by classmates, who also happened to be star athletes of the high school in the small town where they all live. What was supposed to be a night of fun turned into a horrible crime. Two of the football players at the party held the sixteen-year-old victim, Jane Doe, by suspending her in the air over the basement floor. One boy had her hands and the other boy held her feet. They penetrated her with their fingers, which is referred to as "digital rape," they urinated on her and took photographs. They later filmed themselves joking about the assault, referring to her as "dead." The photos were passed around on Instagram and social media pages. When the verdict came in, the rapists were charged as minors. CNN's Poppy Harlow and Candy Crowley received nationwide criticism because they expressed sympathy for the rapists. "These two young men who had such promising futures—star football players, very good students—literally watched as they believed their life fell apart," Harlow said. Crowley asked a CNN legal analyst, "What's the lasting effect, though, on two young men being found guilty in juvenile court of rape essentially?" Where was the concern for the victim? After the verdict was announced, Jane Doe received death threats on Twitter from friends of the rapists and they called her a slut.

 The 24-hour news cycle, along with the scads of feminist sites that have become so popular in the last five years, have illustrated that Stuebenville was not an isolated incident and victim-blaming is out of control, not just in the United States but worldwide.

A movie titled *The Invisible War* chronicles the truth about sexual assault in the military. Many of these rapes happen to men. It is not just a woman's issue. This is a human issue that must be addressed.

If you only listen to the media, you might believe that deep down all men are rapists.

You hear "boys will be boys" all the time. When a man sees cleavage, he is unable to control himself. When a woman says no, she really means yes. These are the messages that we hear too often.

When women are presented as sluts who are asking for it by wearing provocative clothing or having too much to drink, the implication is that men are unable to control themselves. If I were a man, I would be offended by this veiled accusation. I decided to pose this question on Facebook and I rattled some nerves:

"Question for the men: In the 'rape culture' conversation, you are painted as natural predators/rapists. Women are supposed to cover up and act like nuns all the time because you are simply unable to control yourself. Women are angry. We're sick of the slut shaming and victim blaming and we are vocal about it, but I don't see men who are speaking publicly about being called natural born rapists. This IS what people are saying about you—especially if you're in the military. All men are rapists who will rape at the mere glance of partial cleavage, or an arm, or a toe or a strand of hair. If this isn't the truth, where's your outrage?"

I was met with many different responses, and what I found most interesting was that men DID NOT LIKE THIS. Some reacted as if I were accusing them of being this way. No. I am not and was not. Some said they didn't have time to worry about being called a name because they were just too busy living their lives. To be fair, some men addressed this question with a thoughtful answer and didn't take offense. It was not my intention to accuse, but it was my intention to start a dialogue and to make people think about American rape culture and the messages we send—whether those messages are vocalized or if we, as a society, choose to ignore and sweep the ugly truth under the rug because we just don't know how, or don't want, to deal with it.

Here is my opinion about why men are not defending themselves when it pertains to the back-handed accusation that "boys will be boys" and that men are just acting on their primal instinct: because it doesn't really affect their lives in a negative or immediate way. It doesn't hurt their ability to earn money, find a mate or buy a car. There is no real consequence. It's easier to ignore it. This is very dangerous because by avoiding the issue, we continue to place blame on the victim and double standards have weight. Looking the other way is just as bad as referring to the victim as a slut. Yes, it really is.

How long will we as a culture, and as the human race, continue to look the other way when people are sexually assaulted? How many more high school football coaches will cover up a rape because it might hurt the rapist's ability to get into a college? Or the school's reputation? Or the coach's reputation? How many men will sit back and allow a few to portray them as beasts who have no self-control? It seems to me if we are going to tackle the rape problem, men and women need to figure out the best way possible to find a solution. AND THEN WE NEED TO ENACT THE SOLUTION. Ignoring it will not make it go away.

One solution is for more female legislators to create laws regarding rape and how we punish those found guilty of the crime. Kirsten Gillibrand, a Democratic Senator from New York, is working to address the way the military handles sexual assault. Her passion and dedication will effect change that will benefit everyone, and we need more like her, but her road will be a tough one. One of her causes is to allow for a third-party to handle military rape and not the commanding officer.

There have been cases where the commanding officer is accused of rape, and when that happens, the victim has no legal power and often chooses not to report the crime. It is important for women to be the ones to change how we legislate the crime and punishment of rape. Please DO NOT misunderstand me. I believe male legislators can also help move us forward, but they have been at the helm up until now and not much progressive legislation has been enacted.

In 2012, when I signed on as spokeswoman for Rock The Slut Vote, I remember not wanting to tackle this issue because I didn't feel I had any ideas or answers. After becoming more educated on the subject and hearing personal stories, I feel somewhat more comfortable talking about this incredibly complicated issue. I am no expert. But I do pay more attention to what is happening, and I am thinking about ways we can make the positive changes we absolutely need to make.

One thing I would also like to address on a more personal level is a conversation I had with two fathers. Both have little girls. One evening at a dinner party I was alone at the table with these two dads. The Stuebenville trial was in the news and we were discussing it. Both were aware of my activism, and as we discussed what the football players did to the girl they raped, the fathers made an uncomfortable joke. I don't remember what it was, but my immediate reaction was anger, although I didn't reveal this to them. I reminded them they both have daughters and asked how they would feel if this terrible thing happened to their children. Their tone immediately became serious and they admitted that, of course, they wouldn't want anything like that to happen to their girls. As I drove home, I was very upset at the way they handled the conversation. I couldn't believe they thought making a joke about rape—TO A FEMINIST—was an okay thing to do. This swam in my head for a few days and then in a flash, I wondered if I had jumped to the wrong conclusion. It occurred to me that these men might have felt incredibly uncomfortable, and their pathetic attempt at making a joke was really a way for them to avoid feeling so uncomfortable. Here they were, talking to ME, a big mouth, opinionated activist and they just didn't have a solution to offer. Men like to offer solutions—at least, this has been my experience. They had no solution, so they attempted to lighten the mood. I never brought it up again and I will never really know why they made the joke. But it does illustrate a need for better understanding of rape culture and why we must address the unpleasantness head-on.

Many activists who are looking for solutions argue that

parents should talk to boys about rape and to teach them no means no. An article in TIME online came out in March 2014 titled *It's Time To End Rape Culture Hysteria*.[7] The article was based on a study by the Rape Abuse & Incest National Network (RAINN). In the article, RAINN insists that parents already are teaching boys not to rape. They say it is a misguided argument in the effort to reduce sexually aggravated assaults. Additionally, the study found that 90% of rapes that happen on college campuses are committed by 3% of college males. There has been a lot of online conversation about campus rape in the last several years and victims have complained the crimes are ignored by the schools.

So what do we do about it? We talk about it. We keep it in the conversation, and we vote for politicians who either have worked or will work to tighten existing laws and create new ones that will be more effective. We stop asking women what they were wearing or how much they had to drink. I saw a woman activist holding a sign that said, "Why does alcohol excuse his actions but condemn mine?" That pretty much sums it up. As long as the victim is blamed for the crime, we have a problem and we need to create laws so that women are not blamed when they are raped.

***

I posted a blog where the author brought up the point that when a single woman goes on a date with a man she doesn't know well, she sometimes has thoughts or takes precautions that a man would never even have to think about. She leaves information about the man she is meeting next to her computer so that in the event she is killed, the police will be able to find her body if she goes missing. She arranges to have a friend call or email in the morning and if she hasn't answered either by three that afternoon, that is a signal to alert the authorities. When approached by a strange man, she asks herself if that person is going to rape her. She then asks the reader if they follow the same kinds of rules.

The blog made me start to think about my dating experiences and how I take certain precautions, so I wrote a blog of my own and posted it online. I titled it *Women – Don't Get Raped And Killed*. The following is a recreation of the blog, with some alterations:

I have never actually thought about this in a detailed way before and as I started to, I was flooded with different memories. The idea that by simply going out for what would hopefully be a fun romantic evening could turn into a situation where I am raped, drugged, assaulted, murdered or all of the above made me feel angry, sad and resentful. How many of the men I dated had these fears about me? I am guessing none of them did.

When I was twenty-five, I was an aspiring actress and met a man who said he was casting a film that would shoot in Europe. As he strung me and a group of other young actresses along and had us believe this movie venture was legitimate (it was not and that came out later), he made it clear that I was the favorite and was in the lead for the starring role. I went back and forth with him for at least a month. We had long conversations on the phone. They weren't flirtatious or romantic, they were mostly about how I would be the lead and he would describe the star treatment I would receive—fancy hotels, cars and locations. He talked about Italy and France and how everything would be first class. He told me that I was talented and that the Italian financiers would love me. After we met several times in a ritzy hotel lobby & restaurant—the Century Plaza Hotel in Los Angeles—he called me very early one Sunday morning. It must have been 4 a.m., and he told me that the Italians who were funding the film were flying in and wanted to meet me as soon as possible. He really emphasized the urgency and wanted me to drive to the hotel immediately. The meeting was to take place in his hotel suite. In my groggy state, I visualized my dead, bloody, ravaged body and saw the headlines: *Young Actress Killed Because She Met A Producer In Hotel Room*, and *Tragic Murder Of Aspiring Actress At The Century Plaza Hotel*. I shared my concern with my mother, who was aware of what was happening. I wasn't sure if this movie was a real thing. In fact, I believed it was a long shot, but figured that I needed to pursue it because if it was, it would have been an amazing experience, and in Hollywood, you never know what is real. So after discussing it with my mother, we agreed that she would accompany me to the hotel.

We alerted the hotel staff of what was happening. Now, think if this were a man in my place. Would he have been worried? Called his mother? Taken precautions with the hotel staff? Probably not. In the end, this man proved not to be a danger. He was just eccentric. One day, after I hadn't heard from him for a few days, I called and his recorded message stated the film had been cast. That was that. I never heard from him again. There was no film.

This man was very thin and sickly looking. He had a European accent that was difficult to pinpoint and he threw money around as if he had an endless supply. I will never know for sure, but I think he was dying of an illness. I believe he invented this movie scheme to have one last hoorah. He surrounded himself with beautiful women and showered us with Champagne, decadent cuisine and all the compliments a young starlet could hope for. If the situation were reversed, a young man would more than likely not be concerned that an older, sickly woman would kill or rape him.

In my experience, online dating was a waste of time. On the RARE occasions that I met someone for a drink or dinner, I would write down his name, phone number and as much information as I could find with online searches and then made sure that at least two people had the information before I went out. I also made sure to meet the man in a public place and avoided underground/covered parking structures if at all possible—this I do anyway. The enclosed parking structure is a very scary place for a woman. I took precautions before I went out. I did research. When a man meets a woman online, does he do the same? Does he alert his family and friends in case he winds up dead at the hands of his date? Probably not.

The last story I'll share about what it can be like for women is about an evening I was out with my best girlfriend, who was also an actress. We were at a trendy coffee shop in Hollywood that we frequented often. It was after hours and a group of us were sitting and talking. She and I were the only two women in the joint. There were about four or five young men. My friend was talking about how she applied her make-up. The men were interested and paying attention. She is quite beautiful and she was being somewhat seductive and theatrical as she described how she applied eyeliner and mascara. It was clear she had a captivated audience. As she demonstrated the final touch of her make-up routine, I fell into a literal fear spiral of paranoia. She showed the young men how, after she applied lipstick, she would put her thumb in her mouth and would pull it out, so that excess lipstick wouldn't get on her teeth. When she pulled her thumb out, she did so very slowly to the point that I almost crapped my pants. The men were clearly turned on and I was CONVINCED the deal was sealed. This would be the night I would be gang-raped. There was no question in my paranoid mind. If they wanted to hurt us, it would have been very easy. We were in a locked coffee shop late at night. She didn't say anything sexual and didn't offer to have sex, but her delivery—performance—was very sexual and I was **petrified**. Does this mean she was asking for it? Did this performance make her a slut? Did we deserve to be raped or killed because she was flirting and showing off for attention? How would men feel if the situation were reversed—a group of women talking with two men? One of the men struts his stuff or flirts in a suggestive way. Does his friend automatically assume he will be gang raped? Probably not.

Women have a unique circumstance in the world. **We know that not all men are a danger, but we don't know which ones are dangerous**, so we have to be extra cautious. We have a lot more to think about, worry about and fear in the most common, daily situations.

One might easily say, "Well, you should have never been in that coffee shop situation." Who would give a man that same advice? I can actually see men encouraging other men to hang out with a group of women. We happened to be there when the shop closed, and we knew some of the waiters and we were having fun, so we decided to stay. Is that risky behavior? Was our choice to stay a slutty one? And why is it always the woman's responsibility to make sure she is the "good girl" and the "smart girl" who doesn't stay out late or park in enclosed structures???

We have accepted this for too long, and we need to work together to make as many common sense changes as possible. We will never be a society without rape and violence, but we can improve the system and the most important start is to STOP BLAMING WOMEN! Stop putting all the responsibility on women. Men need to take on this responsibility as well, and men need to be vocal to their male friends and to their daughters, and not worry about whether they will be criticized by the unenlightened caveman types who see this as weak. If for NO OTHER REASON, daughters are raped. Daughters are abused. Sisters, mothers, friends, cousins and so on. Be vocal. Talk about it and make sure that when you hear your male friend making a bad joke or making a statement about how she deserved it, CALL HIM OUT. Tell him it isn't cool and you don't accept that attitude. What is stopping you? Fear of being called weak? Fear of being called a wuss? Think about it.

The only way we are going to get some control and reduce the number of rapes is to be informed, vocal and to vote for politicians who prove they are working to make the necessary changes to address these issues. The way to do that is to VOTE PROGRESSIVE. Republicans are having a very difficult time proving they will do anything at all to move the country in a forward direction. They voted against the Violence Against Women Act. They think there is—or try to sell—something called "legitimate" rape and that rape babies are gifts from God. They think rape kits terminate rape pregnancies, and that women have a natural, biological ability to shut down a rape pregnancy. That's a big fat fail. FAIL!

I have heard some people argue that they have taught their sons not to rape. I wonder how they convey that message. Do they simply say, "Son, don't rape women." Or do they explain in detail why it isn't okay to touch a woman if she says no? I'm not a doctor or a therapist and I don't have a son, but if I did, I would try to find opportunities to gently explain what is and what isn't acceptable. I wouldn't care if he said, "I KNOW, Mom..." I would look for opportunities to start a dialogue and instill the idea that if he becomes aware of other guys who are acting inappropriately, he would need to speak up. I would talk to him about respecting women and how doing so enhances his own self-respect. It's a difficult subject and people can be very defensive about it. But it needs to be addressed, and it starts at home.

The bottom line is, we need more progressive women to create legislation that makes it more difficult to get away with violent sexual crime. We need men to step up to the plate and take on the responsibility of sending a clear message to their sons, daughters, friends and family. It's the coward who chooses to say nothing.

***

When I posted the blog on my Facebook page and explained how different it is for women in the dating world, a couple of men who identify as progressive liberals took offense and claimed that it is the women who need to be cautious. I agree that women need to make smart decisions, but again, why is it *only* the responsibility of the woman NOT TO GET RAPED OR KILLED? If you are a man who feels this way, your logic is flawed and slanted toward the idea that men are in charge and women must obey and deal with the fact that men are just going to rape and commit violence and we all need to get used to it because that's the nature of the male of the species. I don't for one minute believe that to be the case and **neither should you**.

I prefaced my post about women having to take extra precautions with "Everyone should read this," just like I would about a climate change or a marriage equality article. The reason I said that everyone should read it is NOT because I think all men are dangerous or clueless, but because some people need to be reminded, and some men haven't really considered what it's like to be in our shoes. Of course there are men who have considered it, and I know there are more good men in the world than there are abusers and rapists. If more men (and women) felt comfortable talking about rape and not getting defensive when the subject is broached, we would make positive strides in finding solutions.

A man whom I had been Facebook friends with for at least a year came on to the thread and defensively made the claim that not all men are rapists, that he doesn't know any rapists and how lucky he is to have a best friend in his wife. He also mentioned that it must be awful for women to be "crippled with paranoia." What? I may be a lot of things, but I am not crippled with paranoia. I could see this was taking a very unpleasant turn. I replied and explained that women aren't all crippled with paranoia, but that especially since Republicans started to attack women's rights and the ability to see more evidence of rape culture because of the Internet, it is important that we are ALL aware and make an effort to improve things. He replied, "Men do speak up, but you cast large nets. You lose credibility by doing so. Good luck to you. I hope you meet better men." See what he did? He dismissed me. He implied that I am crippled with paranoia and he tried to imply that I assumed he was a rapist or a rape apologist. So he belittled me because he was uncomfortable. My internal reaction was *What a fucking asshole!* But I didn't say that to him. Oh my God, NO! I would appear ~~emotional~~ hysterical!!!! This led to a lengthy chat. I made a concerted effort to be clear and say that it isn't about blaming men, it is about speaking up, and then he wrote this: "You just seem to hate men for some reason. So many of your posts are aimed toward me (not sure if he meant to write "men") for crimes committed by a minority of bad people. Your arguments are old. You act as if men don't care about women being raped, or that men need you educating them on Facebook. We have daughters, mothers, aunts, sisters and female friends. We protect them and love them. Your approach is too hateful. I assure you, if someone raped a woman in our family, they would not be long upon the earth."

Wow. Just fucking WOW! According to him, because I believe we need to put more focus on rape culture in an effort to improve what's wrong and discuss various possibilities, this means that I hate ALL men, and I am always blaming him specifically. I also am guilty of filling my news feed with hate. This is the kind of shit that makes me crazy. It doesn't matter that I attempted to be reasonable and not place blame. I am still called a hater and it's just completely juvenile and gets us NOWHERE!

After having that ridiculous conversation, my take-away is that even though he identifies as a progressive, he fears the equality of women and feels that somehow he will be affected negatively. What else can it be? Why would he make this outlandish and untrue statement? If it were true that I was posting so many hateful comments about men on my public Facebook page, I would not have thousands and thousands of followers—including thousands of men. I would be called out on it all the time. No, this guy has issues and unfortunately, he is not alone.

Unions And Voting Rights

The Triangle Shirtwaist Factory

On March 25, 1911, the Triangle Shirtwaist Factory in New York City caught fire and 146 women who were working there under extreme sweatshop conditions were killed.[1]

Most of the women who worked and died in the factory were Jewish and Italian immigrants and were between the ages of sixteen and twenty-three. They endured long hours— usually ten-hour days, six days a week. Workers earned approximately $1 a day. The unfair working conditions led many of the factory workers to go on strike in 1909. Eventually, the women won concessions on earnings but very little else, and employers locked the women in the building during working hours in order to prevent pilferage and unauthorized breaks. They were trapped like rats in a cage. The practice of locking the workers in the building resulted in a horrific disaster when fire struck on the eighth floor just before quitting time. The only safety measures that were available for the workers were twenty-seven buckets of water and a fire escape that wasn't sturdy enough to hold the women who tried to escape.

The firefighters' ladder only reached to the sixth floor. Women on the eighth, ninth and tenth floors jumped to their deaths in order to avoid being burned alive and to be able to provide their families with a body for proper burial. Other women died of smoke inhalation.

Factory employees filled with terror crowded onto a small fire escape. The structure was flimsy and poorly anchored and may have already been broken before the fire. It eventually collapsed from the heat and weight. Nearly twenty women fell 100 feet and died as they hit the concrete.

Years later, Louis Waldman who witnessed the scene, had this to say to the New York Times:[2]

"One Saturday afternoon in March of that year—March 25, to be precise—I was sitting at one of the reading tables in the old Astor Library... It was a raw, unpleasant day and the comfortable reading room seemed a delightful place to spend the remaining few hours until the library closed. I was deeply engrossed in my book when I became aware of fire engines racing past the building. By this time I was sufficiently Americanized to be fascinated by the sound of fire engines. Along with several others in the library, I ran out to see what was happening, and followed crowds of people to the scene of the fire.

A few blocks away, the Asch Building at the corner of Washington Place and Greene Street was ablaze. When we arrived at the scene, the police had thrown up a cordon around the area and the firemen were helplessly fighting the blaze. The eighth, ninth, and tenth stories of the building were now an enormous roaring cornice of flames.

Word had spread through the East Side, by some magic of terror, that the plant of the Triangle ShirtWaist Company was on fire and that several hundred workers were trapped. Horrified and helpless, the crowds—I among them—looked up at the burning building, saw girl after girl appear at the reddened windows, pause for a terrified moment, and then leap to the pavement below, to land as mangled, bloody pulp. This went on for what seemed a ghastly eternity. Occasionally a girl who had hesitated too long was licked by pursuing flames and, screaming with clothing and hair ablaze, plunged like a living torch to the street. Life nets held by the firemen were torn by the impact of the falling bodies. The emotions of the crowd were indescribable. Women were hysterical, scores fainted; men wept as, in paroxysms of frenzy, they hurled themselves against the police lines."

This tragic disaster led to public outrage. Florence Kelley worked with Tammany Hall leaders to create the New York State Factory Investigation Committee. Legislation was created that required improved safety standards as well as spurring the growth of The International Ladies' Garment Workers Union, which fought for and resulted in better working conditions for sweatshop and textile workers. The disaster also gave women another reason to fight for the right to vote.

The Radium Girls

Around 1917, women were hired in radium factories to paint watch dials with glow-in-the-dark paint. The paintbrushes would lose their shape after a few strokes, so employers encouraged the women to re-shape the brushes with their mouths. For fun, the women painted their fingernails and even their faces and teeth. Hey, it was glow-in-the-dark and that's FUN! The women believed the paint was safe.

The U.S. Radium Corporation hired these women and were hip to the fact that radium is not safe to ingest or to smear all over skin. In fact, the chemists carefully avoided contact with the toxic substance, using lead screens, masks and tongs to handle it. Literature on the injurious effects of radium had been distributed throughout the medical community, but this didn't stop the factories from hiring women and using them as expendable employees. These factories could have easily provided the women with the necessary masks and gloves but they didn't, because there were no regulations. Masks, gloves and tongs would have cost the radium companies money—money they didn't want to spend to ensure worker safety. They even *encouraged* the women to put the paintbrush tips in their mouths— KNOWING the radium was toxic!

Was this a case of employers wanting to make employees sick? Doubtful. It's more likely they just wanted product to sell. Glow-in-the-dark watches were used in the military and money was to be made. So what if women got sick years later? It wasn't their problem. Profit was their bottom line.

Women DID get sick. Many women later suffered from anemia, bone fractures and necrosis of the jaw—also known as radium jaw. Radium and other watch-dial companies denied the radium caused these ills. In an effort to keep this information from the public, doctors, dentists and researchers complied with requests from companies to not release the damning data. At the urging of the radium companies, workers' deaths were blamed on syphilis and other sexually transmitted diseases. The goal was not only to distract public attention from the poisoning, but to tarnish the reputations of the women who died—slut shaming.

In 1922, Grace Fryer, a woman who once worked in the plant, grew concerned when her teeth started to loosen and eventually fell out. Her jaw became swollen and inflamed. A primitive X-ray machine revealed serious bone decay and revealed her that jawbone was honeycombed with small holes in a random pattern. The doctor suggested her condition was a direct result of her exposure to radium. Fryer decided to sue U.S. Radium, but it took two years to find a lawyer willing to take the case. Five women who worked in the factory, dubbed The Radium Girls, joined the suit. Their case set precedents including a baseline of provable suffering.[3]

The Radium Girls case enabled the right of individual workers to sue for damages from corporations due to labor abuse, and resulted in industrial safety standards being demonstrably enhanced for many decades.

These two examples from history point out the importance of voting as well as the importance of fair labor laws. Not every business owner is greedy, but enough are, so we need laws in place to protect workers against those who put profits before the people who work for them. The only way to have laws protecting employees is to elect legislators who support workers' rights and not corporate interests.

***

I used to sell industrial chemicals. The company I worked for often complained about the Environmental Protection Agency (EPA) and their pesky rules—rules in place to keep the air and water clean. Their beef was primarily about the fees associated with EPA testing of certain chemicals. Companies that distribute these chemicals must cover part of the fees.

Without labor laws and unions, employers have **proved**

that employee safety is not always a concern. We know that every employer isn't evil, but there is ample evidence that demonstrates labor laws, regulation and worker safety rules are necessary in order to protect the rights of employees.

In 2012[4] and 2013[5] two factory fires in Bangladesh claimed 120 lives. These factories had no enforced safety codes and, as a result, workers died. Companies and corporations will sometimes take advantage of employees when they know they don't have to answer to anyone. They realize it's not always easy for people to find work. Maybe it's because of a poor economy. Maybe it's because many of the workers have little or no education and won't fight because they desperately need their paychecks. Unions are created to make sure employees are treated fairly, no matter what their personal situations are. The corporations that are greedy hate unions. Part of the reason they hate unions is because it stops them from taking advantage of workers, but they also complain that money from unions goes toward political campaigns. The irony though, is that in recent history, corporations were given personhood status by the Supreme Court, making it possible for private businesses, as well as people and corporations from other countries, to donate to political campaigns and not have to disclose how much they give. Why is this an issue? Because corporations usually lean Republican and unions usually lean Democrat. So not only are companies that have no unions more likely to abuse power, they also have a vested interest in backing Republican and, sometimes, even right-leaning Democratic politicians. Candidates and elected officials get money from these companies as well as other perks. When this happens, government is not working for the people—for you. It's working for big business. These companies also receive tax breaks from the government. So while you may be paying 25 percent or more in taxes, they either pay a mere fraction of that percentage or nothing at all.[6] The money unions use to back Democrats is nowhere close to the hundreds of millions of dollars poured into Republican campaigns. This doesn't mean all unions are good and all corporations are bad, but the playing field is uneven and the result costs you, the taxpayer.

Walmart is a perfect example of how your hard-earned tax

dollars allow the retail giant to abuse their employees. Walmart doesn't pay a living wage. In January 2013, ABC News reported the average hourly rate of a Walmart employee is $12.57 an hour.[7]

That equals $26,108 a year for a forty-hour workweek. And that's before taxes. Are you able to live on that? What if you have a family? If you figure a very conservative estimate of rent or a mortgage costing about $1000 a month, you have $14,000 (again before taxes) left for everything else for the rest of the year. That's usually food, gas, car payments, insurance (health, dental and vehicle), water, power, clothes and everything else we need. This doesn't even take in to account fun things like cable, cell phones and recreation. This means a person who works full time at Walmart may need to take another job. It also may mean people who don't have time to work two full time jobs because they are parents or studying or whatever, **will require government assistance** to make up the difference. Food stamps are usually how people make ends meet. Who pays for this? You and me. Walmart takes in billions of dollars while paying very little in taxes. They import cheap goods from other countries, which means less work for Americans, and the American people are paying for Walmart employees to eat.

Republicans like to sing the song of small government and they insist that social safety nets, like food stamps, turn people in to lazy moochers. While there will always be people who want something for nothing, the majority of people want to work for what they have. They take pride in knowing they can support their families and provide the necessities of life—and maybe have a little left over for the fun stuff. To make the claim that Americans are lazy moochers is nothing but a political ploy and an excuse to turn a blind eye to facts. Walmart should take a lesson from Costco. Both are similar companies, but Costco pays their employees an average of $20.89 an hour.[8] They provide more employees with health insurance and the ability to unionize and as a result, they see less employee turnover. And wonder of wonders, they still offer products at competitive prices.

Obviously, this affects both men and women, but it's a

perfect way to illustrate being informed and understanding who to vote for. Politics is a shady business and we all know that just because someone promises to have your best interest at heart while serving doesn't mean they actually do. Keep an eye on them. If they prove to be liars, cast your ballot to vote them out. Our government is broken right now because we as citizens haven't done our job. Hold those in government accountable for the job WE HIRED THEM TO DO. Slowly, over time, things will change if We The People email them, call and write letters to them. It's not perfect but it IS in our hands. The other choice is to do nothing. If you choose to do nothing, explain to yourself how that will in any way help you or this country.

Texas And The Summer Of 2013

In the summer of 2013, Texas saw a sweeping anti-abortion bill and a state senator named Wendy Davis made national headlines because she chose to filibuster the bill (SB1).[1] The filibuster catapulted her into Democratic rock star status and it also did something else very important. It served to wake up even more women to the effort the Tea Party and other conservatives are making to strip women of their rights. Her filibuster garnered national attention and was reported on cable network news.

Wendy Davis announced she will run for Governor of Texas and the conservatives HATE her. One conservative who chaps my hide, Erick Erickson, called Davis "Abortion Barbie" in a tweet and the GOP has embraced this term. They won't call her by that name on FOX "News" but look at their tweets and online posts. You'll see it. A Tea Party misogynist by the name of Rick Atkinson found out Wendy's colleague, Democratic Senator Leticia Van de Putte, announced she will run for Lieutenant Governor and this was unacceptable to him. He had no valid argument as to why she might not be qualified, so he called her "Barrio Boopsie"[2] because her constituency is largely Hispanic.

If you're thinking he's an asshole who fears powerful women and minorities, then we are in agreement. Not only did he insult her based on gender, he insulted every Hispanic person.

The abortion restriction bill that eventually passed closed down many clinics because of the TRAP laws. If a hallway wasn't wide enough or a drinking fountain was in a hallway and might obstruct, the clinic would be closed. Some of these clinics stayed open but are no longer allowed to perform abortions because the ruling says doctors must have admitting privileges to hospitals. If they don't, they are not permitted to perform abortions. Arguments against the bill claimed that the restrictions placed on clinics were not necessary and the abortions that are performed are safe. Not to mention the fact that these clinics offer other services for women such as pre-natal care, cancer screenings and many other procedures that have nothing at all to do with abortion.

Wendy Davis' filibuster was epic for many reasons. She was not allowed to use the lavatory for the entire eleven hours. She was not allowed to sit down or lean on anything. As it was happening, hundreds of thousands were watching her on live feeds online—including me. Mainstream media was not covering the historic event as it happened, but women—people—were paying attention.

Acting as Senate President, Lieutenant Governor David Dewhurst, ruled at 10 p.m. that Wendy had broken the rules of the filibuster by digressing off topic because she was discussing the mandatory transvaginal ultrasound probes forced on women seeking to terminate their pregnancies. Wendy argued the relevance, but because Dewhurst was hell-bent on removing her, she was given a "point of order" and removed from the Senate floor, effectively ending the filibuster. Opponents of the bill crowded the gallery and as Davis was shut down, the crowd exploded with boisterous and raucous protest and chanted, "Let her speak!"

The filibuster continued. As the 12 a.m. deadline drew near, Senate Republicans attempted to vote on the bill. It was at that point that Senator Leticia Van de Putte rocked the freaking house and said, "At what point must a female senator raise her hand or her voice to be recognized over her male colleagues in the room?" The gallery crowd went WILD with cheers lasting roughly fifteen minutes, enough time to block the vote.

Then things got weird. Or, I should say, weirder. It was announced shortly after midnight on the official Texas website that Republicans passed the bill. I remember seeing this just before going to sleep and I couldn't believe it. Watching it was a roller-coaster of emotions and even though no one really expected Wendy Davis to effectively block the bill, it was disappointing.

The following morning, I woke up to more news. The vote that was supposed to have been taken by Republicans happened AFTER midnight—not before. Texas officials broke the law and altered the website time-stamp, but fortunately a wonk who was watching very closely grabbed a screen shot proving the vote took place after midnight. Thank GOD for obsessive wonks!

The bill was killed—at least for a short time. Governor Rick Perry was pissed that a woman was a fly in his misogynist ointment, so he called a second special session and eventually the Republicans got their way, making it increasingly harder for women to get low-cost healthcare in Texas. Many women who wish to legally terminate a pregnancy don't have options. And it's worth noting that Gov. Perry's sister stands to make a fortune because of this ruling. Milla Perry Jones sits on the board of directors of the Texas Ambulatory Surgical Center Society. This puts her in the position to capitalize on the inevitable abortion demand. Thirty-seven clinics in Texas can no longer offer abortion services but the demand is still there. Women will still choose to terminate their pregnancies. This is fact, like it or not. These Ambulatory Surgical Centers will provide abortions, but the prices will be higher.

The other egregious assertion was the false claim that jars of urine and feces were confiscated from the pro-choice protestors. This REALLY pissed me off—still does piss me off because Lt. Gov. Dewhurst LIED and said he saw the jars. There WERE NO JARS OF FECES AND URINE. An interview in *The Lubbock Avalanche-Journal*[3] reported that the Texas Department of Public Safety (DPS) officers said they had not seen evidence of anyone attempting to bring feces or urine into the gallery. Furthermore, officers told the newspaper that the interview was the first time they had heard the allegations.

It didn't stop right-wing media outlets from promoting and then NOT CORRECTING the lie. *Breitbart, Life Site News* and *Red State* all reported the false information on July 12, 2013. As of November 29, 2013, they have not corrected the story. On an aside, I am not here to claim the liberal media is perfect and they have been known to change and alter stories to appear one way, but when they are caught, people get fired. Liberal media will update stories, especially when it changes the story. In this case, we did NOT see the right make the effort to educate their audience with the truth. It is wrong and I don't care how much one may not like something, it doesn't give anyone the right to lie.

Whether or not you believe abortion is right or wrong, it *is* legal. It is a privacy issue, and those claiming they want small government yet insist on government mandated rape (unnecessary ultrasound probes meant only to shame) are being hypocritical. These laws and restrictions are ONLY happening to women. The divide we see from the two parties has increased with the abortion issue. Most conservative, Republican women want choice. We also know from history that making abortion illegal won't make it go away. It will only make it unsafe and dangerous. This effort to oppress women emanates from an evangelical, patriarchal perspective.

Wendy Davis' filibuster served as another wake-up call for women, and even though the press didn't cover that fateful evening, they did cover the story after it all went down. It is becoming increasingly evident that what is trending on Facebook and Twitter is making national news. Keep that in mind as your peruse the Internet. Your shares, likes and comments are noticed. We The People are determining the stories that popular news programs are covering rather than letting them decide what they think we need to know.

Women Have A Message For YOU!

I put the call out on social media for others to explain why they feel it is important to vote. I let them know the focus of this book and allowed them to say whatever they wanted. So, please, don't take it from me, read what these women have to say to you! And take it even further. Ask people you know why it is important to vote. Pose the question online. Allow for differing opinions and if someone argues that it isn't worth it to vote, don't just blindly accept it—ask WHY and remind them that by doing nothing, they are giving away their power by refusing to utilize the voice they have been given.

The following are some of the responses I received from women who answered my call for opinions. I asked them to address you, the reader, and convince you why voting and why feminism is important. I have only made minor grammatical edits. I gave each contributor the option to identify herself in a way that made each of them comfortable.

From Kendra Hutcheson

Why vote? I ask myself this question every election. Many of my university peers often argued that voting was irrelevant in a rigged electoral system; that their voice was only as loud as a grain of sand dropping on a beach. But still, I voted and continue to do so. Why?

I could get up onto my soapbox and talk about the millions women who were persecuted in order to give me the right to vote in America. I could talk about countless women who are discriminated against abroad who would give anything to have a voice in their governments. I could talk about a number of very true and very moving reasons why every woman in America should vote, but I have a feeling you've heard these arguments before. So instead, I'm going to tell you how I answered my university peers when they asked me why I voted: I'm tired of complaining.

Every day, I read the news and I see my rights as a woman being threatened. I post these stories on social media sites, talk them up in my everyday conversations, and generally attempt to spread awareness about the massive amount of bigotry that still exists, unchecked, in our country. But at the end of the day, the most potent thing I can do to exact the changes I want to see in my government is to vote for the representatives and senators who will legislate fairly and without discrimination. Act instead of complain.

While my vote may seem insignificant at times, it is far more concrete and effective than any 'like,' 'share,' or any other method of complaint I might have. My vote is the performance review that keeps politicians employed. They know that, and they respect me for it. They will respect you for it. If enough women come out to the polling booths, politicians will learn that our rights are not to be tampered with. With every woman who votes, it becomes harder and harder for Congress to ignore us. If enough grains of sand come together, they start to dam up and redirect the water's flow into the ocean.

So next election, instead of asking yourself "why should I vote?" ask yourself if you're done complaining and ready to act.

From Ann Werner

I was a child during the 1950s. It was a different world and roles were well defined. There were always those women who broke the mold—some of those women were my relatives. But women like that—business owners, single women who charted their own destiny—were few and far between. I came of age during the 1960s, when things were changing at a rapid pace. I liked it. I liked that women were speaking up. I married young (because I still had a 1950s mindset) but appreciated that I could have access to birth control. Getting a prescription was never an issue and the thought that a pharmacist could deny me a medication prescribed by my doctor was never even on my radar. It just wasn't done.

Because I married young, the marriage failed. There were so many reasons, Vietnam being a major contributor, but in the end, we just weren't suited to each other. I had to work to support my daughter and myself. An electrical supply firm that dealt in home lighting fixtures employed me. The manager of the department and I put together lighting proposals for the salesmen who worked with several large contractors. We worked closely together and it was never like a boss/secretary relationship. He showed me the ropes and I learned a lot. One day, my boss, whom I will call "Dave", was fired. The owner of the company called me in to his office and told me that he was promoting a young man, "Dennis", from another department to replace "Dave" and told me that I was to train him. I was surprised by the request and asked why I wasn't being given the job, since I obviously knew it enough to train "Dave's" replacement. That man looked me in the eye and told me that "Dennis" had a family. I came back with "I'm a single mother! I need to provide for my family too!" It was like talking to a rock. There was no way he was going to give me a managerial position because I was a "girl" (not a woman - you could be 50 years old at that company and still be referred to as a girl), and therefore, not qualified. It pissed me off. So I told him that since I wasn't good enough to run the department, I wasn't good enough to train my new boss, so I quit. To his credit, "Dennis" found out about what happened and he told me he was sorry. Not that he had anything to do with what happened, but it was at least a nice gesture.

A few years later, a roommate of mine applied for a job and came home so angry that I could almost see the steam blowing out of her ears. One of the questions on the job application was the date of her last period. Yep. The company felt comfortable asking her that. She gave them a large piece of her mind and threatened a lawsuit. Interestingly enough, she got the job! Maybe because of the times and the strides women were making guided their hiring decision. Or maybe she just scared the hell out of them.

These are the sorts of things I thought were over. But here we are, all these years later, fighting the same damned battles that we fought and won back in the 1970s. The reason this is happening is because a certain faction has managed to get enough of a toehold in our government, which has enabled them to effectively mess things up for everyone else. And the reason they got those positions of power is because a lot of people stayed home during the 2010 election cycle. A lot of people who were pissed off because the change they wanted didn't happen overnight stayed home in a snit.

It is important to realize that you have power and your power is your voice and your vote. When you see something you don't like, let your representative or senators know. When we have an election, VOTE! It really isn't rocket science. There are people in this world who would give all they have to be able to have a voice in their government. It is your birthright and yet, so many people in this country can't find the time to be informed and to exercise one of the most precious things our democracy has to offer. No, you won't always get your way but at least you will have your say.

I'm 67 years old and know that I'm older than most of the women who are reading this book. I know what it's like to be discriminated against just because I'm a woman. I have seen the strides we made and I have seen them being systematically stripped away. I don't want that to happen to you. I don't want that to happen to your daughters, your sisters, your mothers and girlfriends. I want a better world for all women, and I especially want the women of the United States to be recognized as equal partners in this country. I don't think it's too much to ask. And I don't think we should have to ask for it. It should be ours by right. Since it isn't, we have to demand it. You do that by raising your voice and by exercising your right to vote. So do it!

From Rebecca

Why is it important for women to vote? We could talk about how hard our ancestors fought to get us our ability to vote and how we need to honor them by using it. Or we could talk about how it is our duty as citizens to do so. But everyone should know this and yet, many still don't vote. I believe all of these, and many more, are great reasons to vote. However, I believe all women need to vote because the politicians don't care about your thoughts until you vote for them, and because many of these politicians making laws, that either only or mostly affect women, know little about us. Don't worry, I don't expect you to just take my word for it. A Google search should quickly get you many comments politicians have made about women, and most are not good.

How ignorant of women are some of these politicians? Well, let's look at some quotes. Rep. Todd Akin (R-MO) has said, "If it's a legitimate rape, the female body has ways to try to shut that whole thing down." He even claimed that doctors agreed with him. They do not. Others have recently come out supporting him, like Former Rep. Henry Aldridge (R-NC). He is evidence that some of these politicians don't even understand us from a simple biological standpoint. Yet they will try to make laws that will control our bodies. I don't care if you are pro-choice, pro-life, or whatever. The point stands that they do not understand our bodies, are horribly misinformed of what we are capable of, and yet they think they understand us well enough to regulate us. I have other examples that show this point as well, including a statement from an Arizona bill signed into law by Republican Governor Jan Brewer stating life begins "from the first day of the last menstrual period of the pregnant woman," which is again not true. I hope you get the point, so let's move on.

Some of these politicians believe women are chronic liars, including State Rep. Roger Rivard (R-WI), who stated, "If you're going to go down that road, you may have consensual sex that night and then the next morning it may be rape." Some women may lie about things like that, but to be so light and so general shows a distrust of women. Rick Santorum stated that, "I do have concerns about women in front line combat. I think that could be a very compromising situation where—where people naturally—you know, may do things that may not be in the interests of the mission because of other types of emotions that are involved." He believes women are too emotional, which begs the question what else are we too emotional to do? These politicians pick our judges who have power over our lives. So far they have picked men like Orange County Superior Court Judge Derek G. Johnson, who has said, "If someone doesn't want to have sexual intercourse, the body shuts down. The body will not permit that to happen unless a lot of damage in inflicted, and we heard nothing about that in this case."

These judges don't respect or understand us, and that causes us to rarely get our justice. For that comment, Judge Johnson got a slap on the wrist. He was not asked or forced to go to a class to learn the biology of women or to go to a rape victims meeting to see what rape can be like. His uneducated and incorrect opinions are allowed to survive, and he is allowed to continue using them on future cases. If we do not vote and do not exert pressure, these people will never change their views, they will never see how wrong they are, they will never see things from our point of view, and they will use their biases and misinformation to make laws that adversely affect us.

These politicians don't understand us and what's more, they don't care to. This should be evident from when they held a meeting to discuss birth control and only allowed men to speak. They do not care what we think, and they will not care until we vote and force them to. I don't care where you stand on issues. I don't care who you vote for or why. You can vote 3rd party to show the politicians that none of the mainstream options are good or right. I will honestly be proud of you for doing so. But no matter what you do, VOTE! Vote in every election you can.

The more women vote, the more power the politicians will realize we have, and the more they will care about doing right by us. I may be young, but I will vote to help my gender and my generation in the hope that when my generation takes charge, we can do a lot to fix our problems, including having our politicians respect women enough to listen to us and to care enough about us to learn what women truly are: strong, intelligent, worthy, brave, powerful, and willing to stick up for our own.

From Melissa Weger

I am 43 years old. I was four years old when *Roe v. Wade* became the law of the land. Of course, I was too young to understand any of that. However, as I grew older I always knew that legal abortion was something that all women had a right to.

During the '80s, I became aware that there was quite an uproar against abortion and abortion rights. Many anti-abortion groups began campaigning loudly to end abortion. I didn't quite understand this. Why would people want to end something that took place prior to *Roe v. Wade* anyway? In my mind, what *Roe v. Wade* did was make sure women did not die from abortions. I decided early in my teens that I would always speak up for abortion rights. I've always known that legal abortion was something that all women had a right to.

I'll never forget a conversation I had with my roommate while I was in college; I believe it was 1989, maybe 1990. She had just gotten off the phone with her sister. Her sister was on her way to Washington D.C. to attend a rally in support of abortion rights. Her sister was older than us and passionate that young women become more involved. Her sister said to her, "We are fighting for YOUR rights. You may not believe that people are trying to take away your right to your own reproductive decisions, but they are. Wake up! If we don't fight back, they will win."

Now, many years later, I write to you, the younger women out there. WAKE UP!! The current anti-choice lobby is trying harder than ever to take away your rights. The past two years are full of examples. Hundreds of bills have been introduced, and too many have passed that limit your choice. Choice is important. Believe me, I know. I never thought I would need to make a choice, but I did.

At 23 years old, I found myself pregnant. I was almost finished with college (yep...I was on the 5 year plan) but I had no prospect for a job. The guy who I became pregnant by was not someone I was in a long-term relationship with, nor did I want to be. I knew that I was not ready to have a child. I could not believe the situation I found myself in. What the hell was I going to do?

I went to Planned Parenthood. Despite what the right wing crazies who want to shut down Planned Parenthood will tell you, they did not encourage me to have an abortion. I received counseling from them on 2-3 occasions. I was given options. They gave me information on abortion, information on adoption, as well as agencies to contact if I chose this, and information about what public services were available to me if I chose to keep the baby. The next couple of weeks were the most difficult and heart wrenching of my life.

I never thought I would be in that situation. I was always careful and used contraception. Guess what, it doesn't always work. Now, I had the hardest decision in my life to make. In the end, I chose to terminate my pregnancy. The decision to have an abortion is not a decision I ever thought I would make. However, I did. Each woman has her own experience and her own reasons for choosing to have an abortion. Restrictions on abortion only harm women. Outlawing abortion will kill thousands of women, as it did in the past. Please ladies, wake up and take up the fight.

You don't know when you or a loved one will be in a position that you need to make a very difficult decision. I am grateful that I had the choice. I'll continue to fight in order to make sure it remains that way for you and your daughters until I die.

From McKinzie Aitken

My name is McKinzie and I am 23 years old. First thing I want to say, your age does not always define your intelligence level or wisdom, it only plays a small role. Young minds are the greatest creators of all. So young ones, keep that in mind because YOU, you all are our future.

It's now 2013, these past few years have been terribly sad and disheartening for many reasons. One huge part of this is the lack of motivation and action by the American people (especially women), who are (not) working to make right what is ours: this country. I'm a liberal, and I live in Utah, enough said there. But that's not my problem. You see, the reason America is so great is you can be who you are without consequence, as long as you don't hurt anyone. "An ye harm none, do as ye will." Now days this is not the case. Not only am I demonized as a liberal and a woman a.k.a feminist, I have people telling me my name is stupid (of all things), how stupid, young, naive, brainwashed, ugly, fat I am, among other things because of my age AND gender (they were ignorant assholes too). Whenever I "debated" with someone, 85 percent of the time it was a personal attack and irrelevant to the conversation. We don't have to take it anymore. We women are damn smart, especially when we put our minds, hearts and souls into it. We could—we *would* change the world if we all stood up and stood together for the common good of all.

Women in our society are not looked at that way, even through our OWN eyes. We've been blinded. Our power buried and forgotten. We are the housewives that stay home and cook and clean and care for the children. That's part of our duty. (Yeah, I know, we're damn good at it too). But now we have come to a point to "rely" on men or husbands to care for us, when we have never really needed it to begin with. We have been TAUGHT to need it. That's the order of things, and I am so tired of this thought process. We cannot do this anymore. Women are strong. We are successful. We need to take control of this absurdity, and make it right again. We need to stop letting these old, white, "religious", "educated" bigots control us. Our minds and bodies. Our country.

We women can and WILL change the world for the better if we come together and MAKE it happen. We must be active though; that is how democracy works. Know what is going on. Stay informed, debate, talk and digest a new opinion, think of something contrary to what you BELIEVE without hostility. Be tolerant, have patience, and stay strong. We, ALL of the people, need to quit being lazy, or choosing to remain ignorant because you don't want to deal with it, or "it's boring." It's time to grow up. With freedom comes responsibility. You live here too. You deal with it either way, with a voice or without. Let us leave a legacy behind for generations to come, so we can say to them one day, "I helped changed the world for good and for the equality of all people. I fought for those who were oppressed. I fought for those who wanted freedom. I fought for myself."

We're united as women, united as the people of America and of this world. Let's bring back to America what it really stands for. That means to stand up and speak out. Your opinion is important, so use the greatest gift you've ever been given: YOUR VOICE. Vote.

From Shellie Blevins - Writer/Poet:

Dear young woman and potential voter,

I worry that you are so busy trying to make it in this life that you are unaware of the extent of gender inequality that still exists today. I worry that you are so busy tending to the needs of others that you are unacquainted with your own needs and the political climate we find ourselves in. Not only are you faced with pay inequality, but there is also inequality in health care and in opportunities for employment. The radical right has infested the Republican Party. They desire to take away your right to be pro-choice if that is what you choose (a choice that should be seen as an act of compassion). And ironically, they also want to deny you access to Planned Parenthood and birth control. They frown upon your right to have equal opportunity for employment, to have a career, to receive an education, and the right to justice in the event that you are a victim of attempted rape, rape, and/or domestic violence.

Social media and the activist/hactivist site Anonymous has shown us that there are still adults of both genders— politicians, legal representatives and communities—who are more than willing to look the other way in favor of male athletes, male students, and men in high places who commit rape to unconscious or conscious girls and/or women. And when the victims of these crimes speak out and seek social and legal justice for the vile invasion to their womanhood, their person-hood, and emotional well-being, these communities blame and slut shame them for drinking too much and/or for putting themselves in a situation that makes them vulnerable. These communities justify rape and the treatment of young girls and women as objects—objects that can easily be discarded, discredited and unheard.

What frightens me more is that these radical ideologies of

the right towards women have unlimited financial support by billionaires who are not shy when buying politicians to advance their political agendas. After all, this is the whole idea behind the Supreme Court's ruling on Citizens United and McCutcheon. Eventually, it won't only be members of Congress who can be bought. Governors, mayors, and other elected members in your community could be bought as well. This is why your voice, your vote, is needed so desperately today!

It is your time! It is time for your generation to see the gifts and contributions by women for what they really are—not a weakness but rather a compelling and treasured strength! This is why I believe your talent is not only needed for women's rights, but also for issues such as poverty (6.2 million children live in poverty in the United States), global warming, peace, and the threat of nuclear disaster.

It has been said recently that women are the untapped resource of our time. It has also been predicted that women (who innately are compassionate beings) will save humanity and the world; and so, I call upon you! I call for your contribution! I call for your intellectual compassion! I call for your vote! Never forget that women have sacrificed and suffered immensely for the right to vote! Please do not take it for granted! Your vote and your involvement collectively with other women and men can turn our country (our world) on the just side of history

You are in a unique position with the possibility of more women being elected to Congress and the possibility of a first female presidential candidate. The tide is in your favor and the time to act is now, so please make no mistake: your vote is needed in both the midterms and in the presidential election!

***

This contribution was not originally written for this book. A feminist blogger by the name of Jen Giacalone wrote this for the *Rising Tide* blog and after I read it, I asked her if I could include it in my book. Thankfully she said yes. She stated exactly how I feel in this awesome post.

Practically Feminist[1]

If there's one thing that we can say for sure about the multi-headed beast that some call Third Wave feminism (or is it Fourth Wave now?), it's that feminism often seems like it can be whatever the hell you want it to be. This makes it difficult for us as feminists to speak with one voice about things that are really important. And in the end, it may be hampering practical approaches to improving things. Feminism isn't **an** idea, it's a collection of a lot of ideas, and we're free to argue them with one another. That's healthy. But feminism needs to sort out what it's trying to do. Right now, it feels more like a chaotic, en-masse reaction to attacks on our rights, as opposed to a positive, proactive movement.

When I first started putting my toes in the waters of feminism, I was really only interested in working on legislative activism. I wanted to roll up my sleeves and call state senators and put out useful infographics encouraging people to email their representatives about this bill or that bill. I essentially limited my entire focus to brass-tacks, equality-under-the-law issues. And it made sense to do that. There was, and still is, so much work to be done on that front, and so many legislators trying to take away rights our mothers fought for, that it felt unproductive to get drawn into "soft" cultural issues and wrangling with feminist theory. On my best days, I am a practical gal.

The truth is, though, that it's useful to explore cultural issues and feminist theory because it forces us to reflect on the underlying biases of the choices that we, as well as our politicians, make on a daily basis. Feminist theory is often the soft underbelly of public policy, and its thinking often colors the more "mainstream," legislatively-oriented discourse. The problem is, the continuum of idealistic feminism often yields ideas that don't translate well to the harsh light of day-to-day living. The policy activists and the Judith Butler disciples have to figure out how to talk to each other, because right now, it feels like a food fight: nobody's really getting hurt, but boy is it a mess.

I recently found myself in a real, live argument with a

bunch of other feminists about whether or not sex work is a particularly healthy or positive career choice. Spoiler: my position was, "Broadly speaking, no." I was a little surprised at how unpopular a position this was. I got roundly scolded for prostitute-shaming, silencing, and even being a flat-out misogynist. It was a little mind-boggling that there was more of this than there was actual concern for the very real structural dangers and problems inherent in that industry. It may have been the moment I finally chose a label and slapped it on my sweater: call me a *"practical feminist." "Dear lord!"* I thought. *"Give me back my old-fashioned public policy wonkery!"* I can tell you why we need an Equal Rights Amendment, and tell you whose office to call about it. It's straightforward. But ask me whether or not a girl should take what seems like a few smallish precautions to avoid a sexual assault...? That's a hornet's nest. Many feminists argue that such advice contributes to victim-blaming. I would never have thought that risk-reduction precluded teaching consent. But here we are.

You find these divides throughout feminism on a whole host of issues: Is sex work an empowering life choice? Should we specifically do things to avoid rape? Should someone tell Miley Cyrus to put some clothes on? Someone **besides** Sinead O'Connor? For crying out loud, we can't even agree on how we feel about the relatively unimportant matter of sledgehammer fellatio: is it empowering or degrading? Of course it's Miley's right to do it. Don't be mad though, at the feminists who can't work up much enthusiasm about it.

Women are sexually harassed on the street, ogled at work, passed over for opportunities of all kinds, because for so many men, we can't possibly be more than instruments for their enjoyment. So, when you, as a woman, lead with your sexuality, it can be hard for a lot of people to see that there's a person, with talents, opinions, preferences and passions, attached to it. And it's hard for some feminists to say, *"You go, girl!"* to the woman who's choosing to do it, because it can feel like she's perpetuating the objectification that, in spite of our best efforts to leave it in the past, is still a problem. Short version: it feels a little counterproductive to put your tits in someone's face and then get annoyed when they aren't looking you in the eye. But it's a debate feminism is still having with itself, and nobody really has a good answer. And in the meantime, women and girls are still getting the short end in a lot of ways, large and small.

So practically speaking, what do I think would help it? I like policy prescriptions, so I'm likely to reach for mundane things like accurate and early sex education, a gender studies requirement at the high school level, and with any luck, a loosening of religion's stranglehold on our morality and public policy-making. Despite the fact that the jury is 100 percent in on the failure of abstinence-only sex education, we're still dealing with deeply religious policy makers who seriously believe that simply not giving kids information about sex will keep them from having it. (The irony is, most abstinence education does far more to devalue and objectify young girls than Ke$ha shaking her booty in a thong.)

Pushing for high school health classes to require a unit on consent as part of sex education would do far more to prevent rape than berating women who sometimes circulate those "how to avoid rape" lists. Pushing to decriminalize prostitution is a far more empowering step than demanding that fellow feminists affirm sex work as a positive career choice. Regulated prostitution appears, at least from a number of studies, less dangerous and damaging to the women (and men) in it than the system we have now, and it's a move that a lot of feminists could get behind; why are we expending so much energy policing each others' feelings about it as a life choice, when there are massive, practical, structural problems with it (risk of arrest, STIs, dangerous weirdo clients) that we could be working on? We don't have to give 100 percent approval to everything in one another's hearts; we just have to figure out how to band together on productive actions.

If we're not all at least somewhat aligned on what it is we're supposed to be fighting for (or against), in what sense is feminism a movement? The very nature of the term "movement" is pretty clear. It's supposed to move. Presumably forward. Going backwards, and even standing still, aren't options. If we can't coordinate, we need to at least get out of each other's way. It would be nice though, if we could agree on some concrete things we can DO, together, or else this is just one giant online coffee klatch, and everyone's got a bone to pick. It's human to respond to stimuli, but if the response isn't coupled with a plan, then that's all it is. A response. Not a movement.

There's work to be done, ladies, and a lot of it. Who's with me?

My Dad Is A Feminist

When I was twelve, my father and stepmom, Roz, were stationed in Moscow, Russia and I lived with them for nine months. I attended the Anglo American School and it was an AWESOME experience. My stepmom traveled back to the states in March as she was just about to give birth to my first sibling, my brother Benjamin. My dad and I were alone while she was away.

One day in science class, I noticed a weird smell emitting from my body. It was awful and I didn't understand what it was. I went to the bathroom and when I was doing my business, I looked at my panties and I realized with terror that I had become a woman. I was HORRIFIED. I DID NOT EVER WANT MY PERIOD. NEVER. EVER. I remember reading the book by Judy Blume, *Are You There God, It's Me Margaret.* It was about a young girl who wanted her period. I remember thinking, "What the hell is wrong with Margaret?" I tried very hard to convince myself that is was not blood on my panties and that I had crapped my pants—that's how much I didn't want to get my period. Eventually, I succumbed to the truth, and I remember I had such a dramatic reaction. The first thing I thought was "I CAN GET PREGNANT NOW!!!" Forget that I had never even kissed a boy, I was still completely freaked out by that idea and decided I needed to go home immediately. It was entirely too traumatic for me to finish my school day. I went to the nurse and explained that I was sick and needed to go home. The nurse called my father and he left work to pick me up—not knowing what was wrong. Being the worrying hypochondriac that he is, he had already scheduled an appointment to see the doctor.

Before I go on, I must inform you that the idea of sex, sexuality, breasts and anything having to do with me becoming a woman was terrifying to me. When you looked up the definition of prude in the dictionary, you saw my picture. My father and I NEVER talked about sex. My parents separated when I was three and I had always lived with my mother. I only felt a little bit more comfortable asking her questions pertaining to sex, but my dad?? NO WAY!

When he picked me up and we were in the car, he told me we were going to the doctor. Quietly I mumbled, "I don't have to go to the doctor." He asked why and I explained I wasn't sick. He continued to try and understand why I had insisted on going home and I was too mortified to say it out loud. My mom, my stepmom, and every other important female in my life was in the United States. My dad was all I had. He asked if it was a "woman thing." I answered sheepishly, "Yes." Then he asked, "What is it?" Okay, I knew that he knew and I was irritated that he wanted me to say it. So I stayed quiet. Then he said in a funny dad voice, "Did you get your period?" "YES, OKAY. YES, I did." It was awful. Totally humiliating.

Living in Russia was quite different than living in the U.S., and at the time, many foreigners had beta videotape machines. Family and friends would send us television shows and movies to watch. We had just received a new batch and as soon as I got home, I asked my dad if he would make me something to eat and he suggested I watch *My Fair Lady*. I hadn't seen it, so I was game. We called my stepmom and she explained where all the sanitary napkins were and it was a pretty quick conversation. I was already aware of what I needed to do—peel the strip, stick to my underwear and voila. My dad was great. He made some food and let me watch the movie alone. I was enjoying it immensely and kept asking him to wait on me and eventually, he grew irritated and barked at me. He made a comment that I just got my period; it wasn't like I was dying. He was right. I was taking advantage of his good nature. I felt sorry for myself but after a few hours, it wasn't such a big deal to me.

My dad and I have always been friends. We haven't always

agreed on everything, but I have always known he loves me deeply and would die for me if he had to. He has encouraged me to study up on feminists and was the first person to introduce me to the Triangle Shirtwaist Factory story, and he was also the one who told me about the Radium Girls.

The reason I am writing about my relationship with him is because I have heard people argue that feminists hate men because they had bad relationships with their fathers. I haven't. I have oodles and oodles of stories about my dad being a good, loving man and father. He has encouraged all of his children to be self-sufficient and educated. He's never once made any of us feel that the others are somehow better or more important.

While in Russia, I attended a school dance and he and my stepmom were chaperones. One of the students was a girl who had cerebral palsy. No one was dancing with her. My dad noticed and although his dance moves aren't celebrated by anyone with sight, he approached her, asked for her hand and they cut the rug. It was evident she was having a ball and it was so sweet.

Roz is an Emmy Award winning editor for the news business and I have heard him giving her advice and encouraging her to take risks. The two of them love to talk and laugh.

My dad is an amazing cook. Whenever they have dinner parties, he and Roz both cook and share the responsibility of entertaining.

It bugs me when people who don't know me, but know I am a feminist, accuse me of hating men and having a poor relationship with my father. How dare they make a false and bitter assumption about my private life because I believe women deserve equal stature in the eyes of the law. Like with any family, we've had our share of disagreements, but the love has always been there—no matter what.

Both of my parents taught me to be a strong, independent thinker. My mother is a hard-core liberal. My father is liberal but because he worked in Washington and on many presidential campaigns, he is disgusted with most politicians. He votes Democrat because he's a union man. In the last several years, he's become more partisan as he has witnessed what has happened with the Republican Party.

I've mentioned that in my daily routine, I peruse the Internet for news stories. I look for things to post on various high-profile social media pages. Much of my focus is on feminism, and I am saddened to see so much negativity around the movement. People just don't seem to understand that it's about equality. They turn it into something else. Every now and then, an extreme or militant approach is presented and some people assume all feminists are this way. My father and I were discussing this very subject and he told me a story about when he was a young man in the '70s. The Women's Liberation Movement was in full force and a female neighbor, who my dad was friendly with, was having a feminist meeting in her apartment. He was interested in what they would be talking about and asked if he might attend. His friend told him that he probably wouldn't be invited because some of the feminists might feel inhibited and uncomfortable. He told me that, looking back, he understands why they would feel that way. The women's movement had just taken off and the women felt they needed to figure out their strategy before inviting men along for the ride. Needless to say, he was disappointed. My dad is a real history buff and has been in the news business his entire working life. He has a genuine curiosity and likes to hear and consider different perspectives. He explained that he was disappointed and that by leaving men out of the equation, feminists were doing themselves a disservice and I agree. There are always going to be those who don't understand that as a movement, feminists need to make everyone feel comfortable and that's the whole point. I believe it's only a small percentage who don't get it. Fortunately, he didn't allow those women to color his overall view of feminism in a negative way.

Feminism is a movement, and the majority of women—and men—who wish to see equality are not extreme. They are everyday people. They are not necessarily activists or even very vocal about it; it's just something they believe in.

Negative feminist stereotypes are such a waste of productive energy. It is the same as hating on an entire group of people because one of them is an asshole.

***

It was a warm day in August when I spoke at the We Are Woman rally and my dad wasn't feeling well—nothing dire, but he was having a few problems and tired easily. He stayed to watch me speak. There is a video of my speech on YouTube. Unfortunately, the footage is not great. It's kind of blurry. I should have had my father film it, since he worked as a cameraman for a major news network for over thirty years. DUH!!! But in the video, I can see him photographing me as I am speaking. He was running around, getting pictures of me from all angles.

My dad wants my sister and me to have choices. He wants us to be happy, and even when we disagree he respects my opinion. He believes that men and women are equal and should be recognized as equals in the Constitution. That is a feminist.

Madison

In the summer of 2013, I was made aware of a then twelve-year-old girl by the name of Madison Kimrey. If you follow me on Facebook, you know her too. One evening I was lying in bed and I checked Facebook on my phone. A friend posted a petition by Madison and I asked her to email me the link. I love promoting kids and Madison's petition was an attempt to meet with her governor to discuss a sweeping anti-voting rights bill he eventually signed into law.

Here's what happened: Madison and her mom were at the North Carolina governor's mansion one day at a Planned Parenthood protest. They were there for a while and just after they left, Governor Pat McCrory, came out, handed the protesters cookies and said, "God bless you." The protesters wanted to talk with McCrory but he went back inside.

Later that evening Madison saw a tweet from @OccupyRaleigh that said there were still people at the mansion and Madison wanted to go back. She asked her mother, Mary, and they headed back. Mary suggested they stop first to buy some snacks for the crowd. The crowd of around thirty dwindled to about four or five people and a mansion staffer started to close the doors to lock up for the evening. As a joke, and in reference to the cookies passed out earlier, someone in the crowd asked for some coffee. Madison chimed in and jokingly asked for some brownies. The staffer came back with some cake and handed it out to the crowd. Everyone understood it was all in good fun and when Madison got her piece, she said, "I'd like some rights to go with this." Everyone laughed.

Soon after, the local news station reported that the cake was handed out at a child's request. Madison was pissed. So she asked Mary about starting a petition to speak with him. Mary told her if she did, it would probably get a lot of attention. Moms are usually right and in this case, she was right on the money.

Among the many restrictions in the bill was one that was close to Madison's heart. After the bill became law, sixteen and seventeen year olds lost the ability to pre-register to vote. This is important, because if young people who want to vote turn eighteen on the day of or before Election Day, they will not have the time to register and will not get to vote, even though they are of legal age.

Madison's request was reasonable and fair. She specifically mentioned that this isn't a partisan issue. She just really wanted the opportunity to have a thoughtful discussion with the governor. She was hoping the petition might change his mind. Although Madison still has a few years to go before she is eligible to sign up for early registration, she was understandably upset. She is a gifted and incredibly intelligent girl, and she believes it is her civic duty to be involved in her community and her country.

When I first saw her petition, there were just over seven thousand signatures. I loved her moxie. I love to see young people—especially young girls—stand up for something they believe in. I have blogged about other young women and when I saw what Madison was doing, I was impressed. I wrote an article about her activism and sent it to her. She replied and we became buddies. I discovered her blog called *Functional Human Being*. The first post I read of hers had to do with abortion and the right to choose. Her message was so logical, heartfelt and intelligent. I wanted to scream about her from the rooftops. I wanted the world to meet her. So I did what I could to help spread her message.

Soon after my article, she tweeted to me that she had been busy and included a link to a video she made where she addressed McCrory directly. I watched it and was blown away with how articulate and natural she was on camera. I tweeted back and asked if she was really a forty year-old woman. She replied with "After I made the video, I went and played on the playground." I LOVE this kid! Humor AND smarts! WIN!

My ability to post on public Facebook pages provided her even more exposure. I wanted as many people as possible to know what this young phenom was doing. Pat McCrory was asked in an interview what he thought of Madison's request, and that was when he showed his true colors. He said the notion of her wanting to discuss voting rights with him was "ridiculous" and then he called her a "prop" for liberal groups. In another interview, he said that Madison was at the gates at 10:30 p.m. because she was hungry and asking for food—because he figured if he lied, people would believe him. McCrory didn't take her seriously because she's a young girl. Silly Governor. Within a short time, Madison was interviewed by Melissa Harris Perry on MSNBC.

Why did a United States governor belittle a young person who showed a vested interest in democracy? Could it be that he is bought and paid for by Art Pope? Pope is a wealthy conservative who is working toward eliminating the progress North Carolina has been experiencing in the last decade. Up until the 2010 election, North Carolina was seeing high voter turnouts. It is an important state because it is purple—split between Democratic and Republican voters. Young people have a tendency to vote for Democrats, especially on social issues like marriage equality and abortion rights. By making it more difficult for people to vote, especially young people, the wealthy conservatives feel as if they can hold on to their power a little while longer, or at least long enough to keep their agenda in place. It is unlikely that will happen. The world is moving along and those who wish to halt progress will only find success in the short term. What is funny is that Governor McCrory *is* having a conversation with Madison but he doesn't address her directly, and without even realizing it, he is allowing her to take the lead.

There is an old rule in show business that says if you want attention, never work with animals or children—they steal the show. I have a sneaking suspicion that McCrory knows he will look like a real asshole if he has a sit down with Madison—and he is already up against a lot of angry North Carolinians—so he chooses to dismiss her as a prop. What a completely stupid move on his part. And when I say "what a completely stupid move" I mean he looks like a gigantic asscandle.

McCrory made the mistake of dismissing Madison, and while she would have continued to be a fierce activist and a force to be reckoned with if he had simply ignored her, the fact that he treated her as if her request was insignificant only fueled her fire. Mine too. This is where she and I are similar. In fact, I am only aware of Governor McCrory BECAUSE of Madison.

She continued to post and to blog and then, one day in late October 2013, she spoke at a Moral Monday rally and her speech was filmed by the NAACP. It immediately went viral. In her speech, she said she is the "new generation of suffragettes" and that she is not a prop. Poised and articulate, her message resonated with many disgruntled voters and the following day she was all over social media. There were memes and articles and she was the darling of the political world. Rock The Vote tweeted that she was "epic" and an "inspiration." The day after her speech, she appeared on *Politics Nation* with Reverend Al Sharpton.

Madison will go on to do great things. Before long, she *will* be a household name. She is also an actress, so it will be interesting to see how she grows and what she chooses to do with her life. I have a feeling that society will want her voice in the political realm. Many have already said "Madison for president!!!" We do need more women in politics, and her passion and enthusiasm are contagious.

I am helping to organize the 2014 We Are Woman rally and suggested Madison as a speaker. It was a no-brainer and everyone on the committee said yes immediately! Madison was thrilled with the idea! I CANNOT WAIT to meet her and Mary. We all have similar senses of humor and sass. When I emailed Madison about it, she replied with "I am not sure the world is ready for all three of us together..." Did I mention that I love this kid?

There are some liberal adults who have voiced their suspicion and mistakenly believe it's really her mother or an adult writing for her or planting political ideas in her head. No one does Madison's thinking for her. Period. Madison and I talk. Not all the time, but we have chatted on the phone and we often exchange emails on Facebook—using each other as sounding boards. She'll run ideas by me and vice-versa, we talk about our plans and different events we are involved in. Basically, we talk shop. Sometimes we even talk about boys. She has a sharp and very quick wit. You can't fake that type of thing. And even though most twelve-year-old kids are not interested in politics, some adults sure like to assume they are not capable of independent thought. Worse, those adults are usually the ones complaining that young people aren't smart or engaged.

I was smart enough to ask her to contribute a piece for this book before she becomes so famous that she no longer has time to deal with my requests. Almost everything I have written in here has been my attempt to convince you to vote. I made an effort to not take a dry textbook approach. I have no idea if you are convinced that voting is vital to a thriving democracy. I hope you feel that way, and if I was unable to convince you, hopefully a twelve-year-old girl will. If she can't, I guess no one can. Read her words and think about them. Take responsibility for your country and don't make excuses because it feels easier to proclaim politics are corrupt than to make an effort and participate. If you lived in a house with ten people, your vote would be important and you know it. America is just a big house and we all live here. Your vote and participation counts.

A message from Madison

Here in North Carolina, my home state, the radical right recently put through a 56-page voter ID bill. Many parts of this new law are designed to discourage young voters. The fact some of our elected representatives are choosing to react in this way means we have to keep speaking out. We have to let those who want to silence us know that we will not be quiet.

It's especially important for girls to keep speaking out because all over the nation, laws are being passed that affect women's rights. It's not a coincidence that the same faction of the same party that wants to reduce youth participation at the polls also wants to reduce the number of choices women have when it comes to our bodies and doesn't want to guarantee us equal pay in the workplace.

Each girl has her own voice and her own individual opinions on the issues. When we stay true to ourselves and use our own unique voices to express ourselves, we encourage other girls to do the same thing. It's important that girls know others just like them are taking a stand. Even if we aren't old enough to vote yet, we can make a difference. We can inspire others. We can influence the direction of our country.

These words are from North Carolina's state song, "Hurrah! Hurrah! The Old North State forever! Hurrah! Hurrah! The good Old North State! And her daughters, the Queen of the forest resembling. So graceful, so constant, yet the gentlest breath trembling. And true lightwood at heart, let the match be applied them, How they kindle and flame! Oh none know but who've tried them."

The match has been lit and my fire burns bright.

***

It is the unenlightened individual who dismisses her. It is the jaded, bitter adult who fails to recognize the thirst for progress when it comes out of the mouths of youth.

Not everyone will dedicate their lives to political activism, but everyone should have an understanding of what is happening in their communities, their states and this entire country.

We are the deciders.

That would have been a great place to end this chapter – BUT WAIT! It gets better. In April 2014, Republicans just voted no on the Paycheck Fairness bill AGAIN and Phyllis Schlafly weighed in. She said there should be a wage gap between the sexes because men don't want to marry women who earn more than they do. I suggested that Madison write an open letter to Schlafly. I didn't tell Madison what to say, I simply made the suggestion and woke up the following morning to the mother of all open letters. I posted it on *Liberals Unite* and it went insane. Hundreds of thousands of views and the support and comments poured in. Madison kept emailing me about the different and wonderful things that were happening as a result of her letter. I was thrilled that she was getting attention for something so important, but I am even more thrilled that this young voice is making a real difference. This post went viral and earned Madison her own byline on *Liberal's Unite.*

Behold:
Open Letter To Phyllis Schlafly From 12 Year-Old Madison Kimrey

Dear Ms. Schlafly,

I'm a teenage girl who has been reading about you quite a bit in the news lately. It seems to me that you have absolutely no idea what women of my generation are all about. I can understand that because I often deal with older people who think that their generation is superior and my generation is the worst thing ever just because we're different. Really though, I think since you want to be all up in the public eye, it would really do you a lot of good to understand things from the perspective of one of the young women who will be taking over this country soon.

I've been thinking about how I can explain what feminism means to my generation in a way you might not have thought of before. I wanted to try to work from something we have in common, and it's been kind of hard to find something I have in common with you. Then, it came to me. I bet you wear a bra.

I recently read about a company called Yellowberry, that was started by a young woman because she took her younger sister bra shopping and her sister didn't like any of the choices. None of the bras fit her, and she felt the selections were too sexual. So she started a line of bras so that girls would have more options. As for myself, I shop at Victoria's Secret. It's not because I want to be sexy or have any grand delusions of looking like one of their models. I shop there because they have different styles of bras so I can find something I think is pretty that fits me. I don't know where you shop for your bras, but I bet you have a favorite one. I bet you have that one bra that's comfortable and goes with just about everything. I bet the last thing you were thinking about when you bought that bra was what a man would think about it.

Well, making choices in our lives as young women is kind of like finding that favorite bra. Not all of us are going to fit into the same kind and not all of us are going to find the same style attractive. We all deserve to have as many choices as possible, and as women, we shouldn't be judging the choices made by other women. Choosing a bra is a very personal choice and is none of anyone else's business. We should be, as women, looking for ways we can expand the choices both for ourselves and other women, just as Megan Grassell did when she started Yellowberry. Equality doesn't mean women will all make the same choice. It means women will be treated the same no matter what choices they make.

This brings us to the idea you have that women shouldn't have equal pay because it will make it more difficult for them to find husbands. What you're doing is attempting to limit my choices, and I don't appreciate that. Let's get one thing straight here. When I'm thinking about what kind of career I want to have, it's a lot like shopping for a bra. I want to find something that fits me and appeals to me, and I'm not thinking about pleasing a man. Anyone who wants to be my partner in life is going to have to truly respect me, appreciate me for who I am, and honor the choices I make.

What you're doing, Ms. Schlafly, is contributing to something very disturbing I see happening with some of the teenage girls I know. At a time in their lives when they should be free, independent, and exploring and preparing for the possibilities they have in the future, many of them are worried about getting or keeping a boyfriend. There are young women my age who are extremely smart but they hide it because they get messages from women like you that if they are too smart or successful, boys won't like them. They get messages from women like you that pleasing a man should be their number one goal. You're contributing to making young women uncomfortable when they go bra shopping because they've learned to analyze every choice based on what other people will think instead of having the freedom and confidence to choose what's best for them.

I'm going to continue the work my mother and my grandmothers started, the work you have fought so hard against. I'm going to work to help get the Equal Rights Amendment ratified in my lifetime. Once this is done, it's going to take some time to undo a lot of the damage women like you have caused. It's going to take time for society to evolve once women finally have the equality we deserve. But I believe that my daughters will look at history and see women like you the same way I see women who tried to prevent us from getting the right to vote. I believe that bra shopping is going to be a lot easier for my daughters than it is for girls today.

Sincerely,
Madison Kimrey

Put THAT in your anti-feminist pipe and smoke it, Schlafly! And just know that after you expire, Madison will still be very young and her passion, determination and strong voice will undo most of your dirty work!

From The Men

So, did you notice the page dedicated to men was blank? I asked a few men to contribute to this book. They said yes. In fact, they contacted me a few weeks after I asked and asked me when the deadline was. I told them it was November, 2013.

November came and went and I never received their contributions. Now before I proceed, I'll say this. These particular men believe women are equal and should be recognized in the Constitution and they are activists who are working toward gender equality. These men are **not** closet misogynists, nor are they hypocrites who don't practice what they preach. They are fighting hard for what they believe in. They are busy people—but so were the women who shared a piece for this book. What do you think the difference is?

I believe the difference is this: they are men. They don't experience first-hand what it's like to live as a woman. That's not to say they don't have empathy, or that it isn't important to them. It's just not *urgent* for them—not in the way it is for a woman. Now again, to be completely fair, one of the men I asked is a self-proclaimed feminist who started a new job. He may have forgotten. I specifically told the men who promised to contribute that I wouldn't keep pestering them. I didn't want to be a pain. But I was also curious to see if they would meet the deadline without pushing them.

I'm pro-marriage equality but I don't show up to every rally for that cause. Why? Because it isn't directly impacting me. I'm pro-choice, but I don't show up at clinics to face off with those who are trying to prevent women from receiving the services they need. It doesn't mean that I don't care. It just means that I have other things on my plate.

As I mentioned, the men I approached are working hard so that we can all experience equality, and I respect and admire their efforts. This is precisely why more women need to be vocal—especially younger women. This is OUR fight. This is YOUR future. What happens or doesn't happen today impacts you tomorrow, and it also impacts your children and grandchildren. I know it isn't always so easy to fully comprehend this idea when you're young, but TRUST that I am right. Make the effort. Don't believe for one minute that it'll all be okay and that other people will take care of things for you. In 1917, Alice Paul and Lucy Burns went to jail **FOR YOU!** They did it so that **YOU** can vote and run for office. Choosing to not participate is a big slap in their faces. It's an insult to all those who work hard for the rights of women and most importantly, it hurts **YOU!**

Not All Men Are Sexist! Duh!

I like to play a little game with myself when it pertains to sexism. If a man says something I feel is sexist, I ask myself if it would be just as offensive if a woman said the same thing. If the answer is yes, then I am not so quick to assume the man is being sexist.

Here are two examples:

Man: I don't want to marry a woman who has had sex with a lot of different men.

How do you feel about that? Is that a sexist thing for a man to say? Do you have a different opinion when it comes from a woman?

Woman: I don't want to marry a man who has sex with a lot of different women.

Without a doubt, there is a double standard. Female virgins are valued and put on some kind of purity pedestal, while men can go have as much sex as they wish with as many partners as they wish, and they are seen as manly and virile. However, I see this example as personal preference. People have preferences and it may not always be based on political or religious ideology. Maybe the desire for a partner to have only a small number of lovers is based on sexually transmitted diseases. We don't always know why people say or do things, and we shouldn't assume we know the answer.

Let's try another one:

Man (manager of a mixed-gender sales team): I want John, not Jane, to handle the Acme Golf account.

Could be sexist. But what if a woman who was managing a mixed-gender sales team said the same thing—but she said: I want Jane, not John, to handle the Acme Golf account.

Is she automatically playing favorites? Is the male manager? Not necessarily. Maybe Jane has worked with that account in the past with another company and has produced positive results. Maybe John used to belong to the golf club and has a great relationship with the contact. See how it can be tricky?

Here are some examples of real sexism:
- Women are bad drivers.
- All men are control freaks.
- Only a man should be president.
- Only a woman should be president.
- Men are better at math than women.
- Women are more tolerant than men.

Those examples paint the other sex with a very broad brush and are simply not true.

You are probably familiar with the idea that one may receive ten compliments but what sticks out is the one criticism. This is kind of how it is with sexism, especially when laws aren't there to stop sexist comments and actions from occurring.

I have pointed out how men can be sexist jerks, but I don't want to give the impression that I believe all men are like this. THEY ARE NOT! There are so many men out there who believe in equality. There are men who teach it to their children and who vote for candidates who promise to effect positive change. I don't have numbers breaking down how many of these men exist, but I will go out on a limb and guess it's a majority—and this includes some conservative men.

There will always be men who make sexist comments. Human beings are imperfect. We don't always say and do the right thing. Sometime we act like assholes, and that includes women. All of us do this. No one is exempt. This is so important to keep in mind. It is very easy to blame and point fingers when we are upset about something. I am angry that the Equal Rights Amendment isn't ratified. I could spend all of my time looking backwards and hanging on to what happened then. I could let it stop me and say, "What's the point?" I prefer to take action and do what I can to ensure a future where women and men have a constitutional guarantee of equal protection against discrimination.

We always need to analyze our own behavior, especially

when we haven't reached our goal. We need to determine what has worked and what hasn't, and then we need to form a new plan that moves us forward. When we are stalled, we need to raise a little hell—or a lot of hell—to get the wheels turning.

The most important thing we can do is create laws that will be fair to everyone. Does that mean everyone will follow the laws and life will be perfect? No. Of course not. When men are not allowed to discriminate against women in the workplace and are held accountable if they do, there will be less discrimination. And the same goes for women who discriminate against men.

Headlines

In 2012, President Obama was reelected. Sixty-seven percent of single women voted for him. We saw many new women in Congress. There was a feeling of relief and the possibility that the batcrap crazy legislation against women's rights was at the very least, going to slow down. HA! No such luck. It seems the volume was turned up. This chapter is a collection of headlines beginning in March to May, 2013.

Women need to get up off their asses and VOTE in every election. If we don't we'll just see more of this.

1. Abortion: Could GOP Bill Prevent Rape Victims From Accessing Emergency Contraception?
River Front Times Blog. March 12, 2013

2. Texas State Senator: Close Abortion Clinics Because Sometimes Men Have Anal Bleeding
The Raw Story, March 20, 2013

3. A New Way To Screw Unionized Women Teachers In Michigan: A "Pregnancy Tax"
Daily Kos March 21, 2013

4. North Dakota Lawmakers Approve Strict Abortion Laws, Setting Up Costly Battle Over Roe v. Wade
The Washington Post - Associated Press March, 2013

5. How Kansas' Anti-Abortion Bill Launches A Sweeping Attack On Women's Rights
Think Progress. March 20, 2013

6. Abortion Opponents In North Dakota Block Comprehensive Sex Ed For At-Risk Youth
Think Progress March 19, 2013

7. North Carolina Protesters Tell Anti-Abortion Republicans: 'You Don't Walk In A Woman's Shoes'
Think Progress. March 21, 2013

8. Anti-Marriage Equality Bishop: 'Sexual Abuse Does Not Happen' In Straight Marriages
Think Progress. March 27, 2013

9. New Laws Ban Most Abortions In North Dakota
New York Times. March 26, 2013

10. Kansas Republicans Mock Rape Exceptions For Abortion Restrictions As 'Little Gotcha Amendments'
Think Progress. April 2, 2013

11. Rep. Amash: 'More sensible' to ban abortions after three days and 'certain' birth control
Raw Story April 2, 2013

12. Ken Cuccinelli Fights To Keep Sodomy Law On The Books
Buzz Feed April 3, 2013

13. Inmate Claims Activist Hired Him To Firebomb House (of a doctor who performs abortions)
San Francisco Chronicle April 3, 2013

14. Nevada Lawmaker Receives Death Threats After Talking About Her Abortion
Think Progress April 4, 2014

15. Missouri Lawmakers Pass Bill Allowing Pharmacies To Nix Contraception
CBS News April 4, 2013

16. Air Force General Defends Overturning Sexual Assault Conviction By Blaming Victim
Think Progress. April 11, 2013

17. Paycheck Fairness Act Vote Blocked By House GOP
Huffington Post April 11, 2013

18. In Just Three Months, States Proposed An Astonishing 694 Provisions About Reproduction
Think Progress April 11, 2013

19. Paul Ryan On Abortion: 'We Want A Country Where It Isn't Even Considered'
Huffington Post April 11, 2013

20. Peter Hansen, New Hampshire Lawmaker, Calls Women 'Vaginas' In Email To Colleagues
Huffington Post April 16, 2013

21. New Mexico GOP Official Calls 19-Year-Old 'A Radical Bitch'
Think Progress April 24, 2013

22. Air Force General Blames Increase In Military Rape On Hookup Culture
The Daily Beast May 8, 2013

Sometimes I Just Want To Give Up

I often wonder why I choose such difficult paths in my life. I pursued an acting career. Because that's so easy, right? When I walked away from it, it was because I just didn't want to do it anymore. I didn't feel like I had failed. I was still young, and perhaps if I had stayed with it, I would have carved out a nice career. Initially, when I left the acting studio I had attended for eight years, my plan was to go back after I was rested and refreshed, but the thought of sitting in another agent's or casting director's office made me want to vomit. So I decided to go into sales and live a more normal existence. The thing is, the kind of sales I chose was the most difficult way to earn a living. I wanted to be an outside sales representative. I didn't want to check into an office every day. I wanted my home to be my base and for a decade, I did just that. I was fortunate to start my outside sales career with a family owned business, Herman Dodge, and I sold coffee and tea related products. I received a salary—even though we called it a draw against commission—and I never had to pay anything back, which is very rare for a commission based sales job. The family I worked for understood it would take time for me to get my legs. I was also sharing my territory with a few other reps who worked for a company that dealt with many wholesalers. When I finally took over the entire territory, I was making more than my salary. I was there for four years, so I did catch a break from the usually difficult path of outside sales. When I quit Herman Dodge to expand my horizons and my earnings, I worked for several other companies and wanted desperately to find a home. I found that in many cases, a company that is looking to hire will say a rep should be able to make a certain amount per year, but reality told a different story. I became a job hopper, something I really didn't want to be.

In 2005 I found a home with an industrial chemical company and it was there I learned that I am a good salesperson. In fact, I was one of their top salespeople. I was very spoiled and had it easy at Herman Dodge. It was not easy selling industrial chemicals. I had to hunt for business with little help from my employers. I enjoyed hunting for my customers. I learned how to bypass the "gatekeeper" and literally go in through the back door or the door that read "Authorized Personnel Only." If I was stopped and asked what I was doing there, I would answer "I'm here to see Dave in maintenance." Half of the time, there actually was a Dave and when there wasn't, the person would usually ask, "Do you mean Rob?" and I would be escorted to the office I was looking for. It was fun and, like some kind of treasure hunt, I would often find the pot of gold and I felt empowered.

I was making more money than I ever had and I really loved my job, although I didn't like that I was working with chemicals that could damage the environment. We sold some environmentally friendly products and as the standards changed, we did away with some of the more damaging chemicals. The fact that I started at zero each month was a bit frightening but somehow, I managed to succeed. And then in 2006, things changed. The economy started to slip. It wasn't fully evident at that point but it was happening. Two of my most lucrative customers fell away. One was the California Transportation Department. They lost significant funding and they had been my bread and butter. They would give me huge orders, and I served many maintenance yards across the Los Angeles basin and surrounding counties. The other was the City of Los Angeles. When the procurement department figured out they were spending three times more than they needed to by purchasing products from me, they put a halt to sales. Rat bait done me in. Freaking RAT BAIT! They found out they could buy the same product at a big box store for a fraction of the price. Procurement sent instructions to all of the city yards that they were no longer permitted to buy anything from the company I worked for. This put a serious dent in my earnings.

Just around the time I lost that business, a headhunter who was looking to fill a position at a janitorial supply company contacted me. After a long courtship, I quit industrial sales and took my chances with a company that offered a great salary plus commission for the first full year. It was a safer route for me and I figured it didn't matter what I sold, as long as I was able to earn a good living. I was happy— for five minutes.

I spent many a hot afternoon in urinals explaining to janitors who hated me how they could clean a bathroom. That was fun. Not. You can imagine how the janitors looked at me; a tall blonde with dangly earrings and open-toed shoes (my sales rep uniform). You could practically read "Fuck you, bitch" in their eyes. The worst were the women janitors. They pretty much wanted to see me dead. It was quite evident in the way they reacted to me, and I guess I can't really blame them. I didn't fit in with that crowd. They looked at me and made assumptions. They didn't expect a woman who looked like me would have anything in common with them. The few who gave me a break realized that I am not a hoity-toity type and that I can and have hung with most anyone.

I tried very hard to like that job. I had some great bosses, male conservatives by the way. Funnily enough, those bosses were some of the most fair and wonderful managers I have ever had. They made an icky job bearable, and I was always thankful for the way they managed the Los Angeles branch. I actually did well, and in my short tenure, I signed on some big customers, including a few school districts. The smelly urinals were gross, but what broke me was an account I inherited—a college—and the lead custodian would inform me he wanted me there at 5 a.m. on random days. The college was over an hour away from where I lived and it meant I would have to wake up at 3 a.m. and this is where I drew the line. I love sleep. I need sleep. I was not told this would be part of my job description and worse, it was all at this custodian's whim. I didn't have a set schedule that I could even get used to. It was random. I HATED it. He was a jerk too. He treated me like a silly girl who didn't know what she was doing. If I met with him and my male boss was with me, I was invisible to him. He never addressed me, unless it was a subtle condescending remark.

Eventually, I quit. I was sad, I had really wanted to make that company my home and even though I justified standing in disgusting urinals with the idea I was making public restrooms a better place, it just wasn't me. To this day my mother can't believe I worked that job. The janitorial supply job taught me that what you sell IS important!

After two more attempts to find a home in sales, the economy tanked and I was petrified. I ended up selling oil—a new low for me. I needed to earn money and the job market was beginning its decline. I worked for a small oil and fuel distributor, and we were unable to compete with the two larger oil distributors that provided the exact same product for less money and same day delivery—something we could not do. I tried very hard, but even when I worked with my boss, who said to me, "I'm going to show you how it's done," he was so defeated after working my territory (downtown Los Angeles), he told me to not even try. There was no denying we were unable to compete. What the hell would I do??? I didn't want to job-hop anymore, I knew that things would get worse before they got better. I needed some time. My mother had moved to northern California. So I decided that instead of looking for yet another job in Los Angeles, I would move up north to be closer to my mother and look for a job there.

Almost as soon as I arrived, the manuscript we had been working on for years, *The Virgin Diaries*, was completed and we wanted to get it out into the world. In April of 2010, we did just that. The book was released and Facebook was just starting to see public "Like" pages. So I started one for the book and I also started a new, personal one where I started friending all sorts of people I didn't know. Being an author is not easy. Surprise!!! Especially if you want to earn money. Especially when no one knows about your book. So, there I was—again—trying to climb up a brand new mountain at 41 years old. I climbed and climbed. It was scary and horrible and wonderful and exciting.

In 2011, the chemical company I worked for in Los Angeles asked if I would work for them again. I was surprised because the owners were really pissed when I quit in 2007. In fact, they never spoke to me when I announced my resignation. I only communicated with my sales manager—she didn't want me to tell them; she wanted to be the one to break the news. I agreed to return as an employee and it turned out to be a horrible disaster. HORRIBLE. A very long story, but the short is the territory I took over in northern California was never successful for any sales rep—I found that out after they rehired me. It is like the black hole for sales; a real boys club and a limited number of businesses to choose from. Not to mention the fact that two school districts I had been working hard to get into our system as customers both lost funding and had to close schools and lay off teachers. I literally drove around for two full weeks and sold nothing. The damn job cost me money because I had to pay for gas. I would come home from a day of being rejected by everyone and I would just cry. Eventually I gave up and worked with the handful of customers who did order from me. I filled in with some part-time gigs.

Then, my life changed again. I got the fated email from Susan Emry. I was still on Facebook promoting myself as an author when she asked me to be the spokeswoman for Rock The Slut Vote. I jumped in and loved it.

Guess what? Being an activist is freaking hard and scary and I don't earn any money doing it—in fact, my savings was exhausted. But I love it—more than anything I have ever done, including acting.

What I have learned so far in my journey is there are two kinds of feminism. There is social feminism and political feminism. The two are often intertwined, and I believe the disagreement on what is feminist and what isn't is what hurts the movement.

If you are stuck on the word "feminist" as a negative, ask yourself why? Stating you are a humanist isn't going make misogynists see the light. You are actually giving power to those who don't see men and women as equals by distancing yourself from the word. THE WORD. Are there asshole feminists? Sure there are. Any type of person can be an asshole, but why would you allow a few assholes to dictate what you will or will not embrace?

Political feminism is about what laws exist in our society that pertain specifically to women. Does a company have the legal right to deny their female employees birth control coverage on company insurance plans based on the religious beliefs of the company's owners? Does government have the right to dictate that a woman must get a vaginal probe before a legal abortion? The political aspect of feminism is more cut and dried. You believe it should be one way or the other. Then, you vote.

Social feminism seems to be the more confusing dilemma. People argue about chivalry or who pays for a date. This falls into individual preference, and it is my opinion that anything goes. Some women don't want a man to hold a door or pay for a dinner date; others do. I'll bet most heterosexual women enjoy when a man makes an effort to impress them. I know I do. I don't have a problem with a man who asks me on a date and pays for the evening's entertainment and holds a door open for me. There are some who argue that a man who holds the door for a woman is really sending a message that women can't do for themselves. I beg to differ. It's called being polite. Occasionally I hold the door for people—men and women, old and young. I do it because it is polite. I also feel that if I were to ask a man out, I should offer to pay because I think that is fair. I have some girlfriends who believe the man should always pay, no matter who asks whom. That is their opinion, their preference. I don't think there is a right or wrong. But I do see people get very angry and fight about these things. Why? Why can't we agree that individuals will live their lives the way THEY want to? Yes, it's confusing. LIFE is confusing. Individuals in each relationship can and will figure out what works for them. The arguing and the judgment is not only a waste of time, it IMPEDES PROGRESS. It makes it easier for opponents of feminism to chip away at what it really means to be equal in the eyes of the law and protected against gender discrimination. That IS what this is all about.

Here's what I believe: the first and most important aspect of women's equality is legislation. If we are able to secure legislation that creates a completely equal and fair country, we will see societal changes. We will see less discrimination. It won't eradicate it, especially when religious law dictates that women are not of equal value to men. Remember though, religious law has no place in the country's lawmaking. The authors of our Constitution were very clear about that. There is no way to legislate an individual's thoughts or beliefs, but laws influence our actions and determine if societies evolve, stagnate or regress.

As a blogger and admin for Facebook pages, I have learned much. I have learned that when I write about political feminism, everything is hunky-dory. When I write an opinion piece about feminism, some people agree with me and other people who have different ideas about social feminism HATE ME and tell me what an asshole I am. In the end, I just want equality and fairness for all, and even though I may disagree with a point of view and may argue against it, there is beauty in our differing views and I have learned to adjust my thinking on occasion because of the differences.

An example of some of the stupid, waste of time things I do see: I can post a funny meme on a page to take a break from women's issues, like the one I posted on Rock The Slut Vote that said chocolate is from a plant and therefore a salad. I thought it was funny. A woman saw it, freaked out, and read into it that it was some conspiracy against women eating chocolate. I'm sorry—but please calm down. There was no mention in the meme about gender. It was a funny meme. It wasn't about women and society's message that women need to be underweight to be considered attractive. These kinds of outbursts are not helping. I see things like this every day. All the time.

When I blog an opinion piece on the social aspect of feminism, before I hit publish, I feel the acid in my stomach start to churn. I know it's going to piss many off—even if I feel it is common sense. I know some people will agree with me and others will disagree and that is perfectly fine, but I also get such rabid hatred coming from some feminists who disagree with me. I disagree with a lot of people. For instance, I love HBO's *Real Time with Bill Maher*. I watch it every week and miss the show when it's on hiatus. There have been many times I disagree with him but I don't sent him hateful messages. I get that we are all have our own points of view and they often differ but why hate? Why jump to anger? There's always that group you can never please. That group who says only women should be the ones in charge of the world. That women should support all women no matter what—yet those very women attack women with whom they disagree. There are the ones who say women shouldn't see motherhood as a woman's greatest accomplishment—who insist women should be in the workplace and men should fuck off. Yes, there are *some* angry women and they will HATE me for writing this. They exist. They are a minority, and for some reason have a starring role in the movement because opponents of feminism love to take extreme examples and present them as the norm. What I consider to be extreme or angry is just my opinion and not necessarily representative of anyone else. I have thought long and hard about all the different kinds of feminists there are and when I first jumped into activism, I believed the extreme feminists were hurting and not helping the cause. While I still believe that extreme feminism can be a turnoff to many, it is precisely how women have overcome the obstacles placed in our paths. Agitation works.

Take a look at the Russian punk rock band, Pussy Riot. If you are not familiar with them, they are a group of mostly women who fight against the Russian Orthodox Church and the country's leader, Vladimir Putin, whom they and many others regard as a dictator. They stage guerrilla performances meant to cause a commotion. When the group attempted to perform in Moscow's Cathedral of Christ the Savior, they were arrested and the world became aware of their actions. One of the band members commented that you can't start a revolution by just asking or being polite. I watched the HBO documentary *A Punk and a Prayer* and it really made me think. It made me realize the importance of risking ridicule and showing the world you are angry. It made me realize that although a lot gets done in the middle—where we can find common ground—someone has to be the first to make a stink. These activists sat in a Russian jail for two years, and as soon as they were released, they immediately went right back to what they were doing. They choose to stay in Russia and fight. In fact, they decided to perform at the Sochi Olympics in 2014. Russian Cossacks attacked them with pepper spray, horse-whips and batons. Talk about bravery! When I look at what I have done, I feel like a piece of dust blowing in the wind. I cannot say I have their courage. Maybe if I were younger and living in Russia I would, but I seriously doubt it. They risk violence and death to open the eyes of others, and while they may not be the ones to change the way Russia treats its citizens, they are definitely pioneers.

Some people may see them as unsavory because they use the word pussy and specifically because of how they treat religion. I thought about what they have done and my first reaction was that they are too extreme. However, as I continued to think about it, it occurred to me that these women are like the American suffragists who went to jail for what they considered to be oppression. In the early 1900s Alice Paul was viewed as extreme as the women of Pussy Riot. Extremism is mostly a perspective. I may seem extreme to some and others may feel that I am not extreme enough. The members of Pussy Riot set an example for people all over the world and I salute their efforts. I bow in awe and gratitude.

***

Feminism is supposed to be about choice—not only reproductive choice, but all choice. Hey, it's great to get positive feedback and it sucks when people fly off the handle and say I am a not feminist enough, but who cares what people say to me? The goal is equality for all. To those who mistakenly believe we have nothing more to fight for and that we are already equal, I say this: WE ARE NOT. Until Women are recognized as equal in the Constitution, there is still work to be done.

So I ask myself, why do I do this? Why do I set myself up for ridicule? Why do I want to stay on a path where some people in the very group I am trying to move forward, at my own expense—both emotionally and economically—say I'm an asshole? Of course, most don't think this, or I wouldn't be writing this book. I do get more positive feedback than negative, and it is important to note that the majority of people on the RTSV page are really cool. I learn a lot from their commentary. A LOT! Negative comments are the ones that sting—even if they have nothing to do with me personally. Those are the ones that stick out, but I learn from all of it.

I keep doing it because I am driven, and because I know the majority of people just want to be happy, healthy and have a good life. I want to see this country move forward in every area and especially in women's rights. Sometimes I wonder if that's even possible anymore. But every day I wake up and do it all over again. I hate it. I love it. I hate it. I love it. I hate it. I love it.

That is why I do it, despite the difficulties. Because I love you. Yes, you. You are a fellow human being and you deserve to have someone fight for you, even if you don't like me or my cause. Even if you are conservative and think I am a baby-killing whore or a champion of evil. I will fight for your right to have choice. I will fight for your right to earn equal pay, and I will fight for your right to choose to be a working professional or to be a stay at home mom.

"If you sexist me, I will feminist you." ~ Author Unknown

What You Can Do

There are things you can do to make a difference—even if the outcome is not what you originally envisioned. You can make sure your voice heard in the voting booth. You can call politicians and let them know what they need to do in order to win your vote or keep their seat. You can spread information via social media. You can engage with others to help broaden your thinking and open yourself up to ideas that you might not otherwise have considered.

One thing is for sure: if you choose to do nothing, your thoughts, hopes and desires for this country are wasted and will only live in your mind. It is a lazy coward who claims to have no power. Power doesn't always mean winning. It doesn't always mean you get your way. It is a process, and sometimes change doesn't occur in the timeframe you have deemed adequate.

What if Alice Paul and Lucy Burns thought, "Screw it, trying to get a constitutional amendment that allows women to vote is just too damned hard. Let someone else worry about it." You might be watching the men vote and make laws while you sit there with no power. That would suck, wouldn't it? But lucky for all of us, those two women, along with so many others, cared about YOU. They cared so much they risked their lives so women they would never know would have to ability to have a say in how their country works. Alice didn't say, "All politicians are corrupt, so who cares?" She went to jail for you. She survived solitary confinement for you. She went on a hunger strike for you. Just knowing she did that for me makes me feel that I need to do my part. I need to show up and vote. I need to fight for equality and I need to tell my friends—even when they don't want to hear about it. I want women in America to be recognized in the Constitution. I am willing to fight for that, even if I don't see it happen in my lifetime. I know I am part of the process. My actions make a difference and so do yours.

Feminists must always be remembered. We come in all packages. Some of us are quiet. Some of us are loud. Some of us are extreme and some of us feel that compromise is the way to go. No matter what kind of feminist you are, you matter. You help. As long as you believe women are equal and deserve that guarantee from the federal government, you are a feminist. The word isn't dirty and it isn't something we need to change. Embrace it, even if you don't want to shout about it from the rooftops.

One day, women <u>will</u> see the Equal Rights Amendment pass, and it will be a beautiful day. It won't be the end of feminism, but it will be a gigantic stride in the ongoing movement. Feminism is, and should be, a celebration of the female spirit and the unique strength that women possess.

I want you to vote. Period. I also want you to think about feminism and why it is important not to discount the word. I want you to really think about the actions and risks women have taken to get us where we are today. Even though American women are fortunate compared to other cultures, I want you to be angry that we STILL don't have full, guaranteed constitutional equality. It is our right. Now let's TAKE IT! Because the Equal Rights Amendment isn't going to ratify itself.

"Deeds, not words."
Dr. Alice Paul

Visit my website:
KimberleyAJohnson.com
Like me on Facebook : Kimberley A. Johnson (Author)
Follow me on Twitter @AuthorKimberley

And don't leave out the extra E in Kimberl<u>e</u>y!

Bibliography

Herstory
1. National First Ladies' Biography
First Lady Biography: Abigail Adams
2. American Magazine
Rewriting History: Alice Paul's Battle for the Ballot
November 2010
3. Magazine of Pacific University Pacific
The Three Waves Of Feminism
Fall 2008
4. The History Project Of UC Davis
Ideas And Strategies Of The Woman Suffrage Movement
5. Biography.com
Harriet Tubman
6. Biography.com
Sojourner Truth
7. Biography.com
Gloria Steinem
8. Ms. Blog February 2012
Black Herstory: The Founders of the Feminist Party

Girl Power
1. The Charleston Gazette April 2013
'Slut-shaming' at George Washington High?

1968 – 2012: My Political Evolution
1. UCLA Newsroom January 2001
Supreme court fails to argue recount ruling
2. FactCheck.org February 2008
The Budget and Deficit Under Clinton
3. The New York Times May 2009
Reagan Did It
4. FactCheck.org April 2013
Obama's Numbers

When I Became A Slut
1.US News & World Report October 2012
Pharmacists Can't Be Allowed To Deny Women Emergency Contraception
2. Huffington Post January 2014
GOP Congressional Candidate Dick Black Doesn't Have A Problem With Spousal Rape

The Anti-Feminist
SOURCE: University of North Carolina at Asheville
A Reason to Fight: The Opposition to the ERA in North Carolina
A Senior Thesis Submitted to
The Department of History
In Candidacy for the Degree of
Bachelor of Arts
November 2005
1 Donald G. Mathews and Jane Sherron Dehart, *Sex, Gender, and the Politics of the ERA: A State and the Nation* (New York: Oxford University Press, 1990), 71.
2. Slade, *The Fraud of the ERA,* folder 662.
3. Elizabeth Carter Harrison White to Senator Samuel Ervin, JR., 24 February 1977, folder 885, *Ervin, Samuel J. Private Papers,* Southern Historical Collection of Chapel Hill, Chapel Hill.

Religion And Women's Reproductive Rights
1. *Wikipedia Deism*
2. Guttmacher.org June 2013
NEW WAVE OF LAWS SEEKS TO SHUT DOWN ABORTION PROVIDERS
3. US National Library of Medicine National Institutes of Health 2005
Abortion in the United States.

Suffrage and Voting
1. Scientific American June 2008
Hedy Lamarr: Not just a pretty face

2. Mother Jones July 2012
UFO Sightings Are more Common Than Voter Fraud
3. Huffington Post August 2013
Colin Powell Condemns North Carolina's Voter ID Law

Why Vote?
1. Think Progress May 2013
UPDATED: Virginia GOP Nominee For Attorney General Introduced Bill Forcing Women To Report Their Miscarriages To Police
2. The Washington Post November 2013
Herring wins Virginia attorney general race, elections board announces
3. USA Today June 2005
Judge upholds Washington governor's election
4. Salon.com   December 2013
Women's rights sold out again: McAuliffe's betrayal
5. Think Progress October 2013
Supreme Court Smacks Down Ken Cuccinelli's Sodomy Law Appeal
6. Think Progress May 2014
Virginia Governor Takes The First Step Toward Repealing 'Extreme' Abortion Clinic Restrictions

Talking to Politicians
1. Liberals Unite April 2013
GOP State Senator Phil Williams Mocks Women In Tweets

Mad As Hell
1. Huffington Post May 2011
Scalia: Women Don't Have Constitutional Protection Against Discrimination

Feminist: The Other "F" Word
1. The United States Census Bureau   September 2013
Income, Poverty and Health Insurance Coverage in the United States: 2012
2. The Guardian June 2013
Susan Sarandon: 'Feminism is a bit of an old-fashioned word'

3. The Broad Side July 2013
An Open Letter to Susan Sarandon on Feminism

Rape
1. Think Progress December 2013
Michigan Lawmakers Considering Abortion Bill That Would Force Women To Buy 'Rape Insurance'
2. The Wire August 2012
31 States Allow Rapists Custody and Visitation Rights
3. Department of Justice January 2006
Extent, Nature and Consequences of Rape Victimizations: Findings From The National Violence Against Women Survey
4. Centers For Disease Control 2012
Sexual Violence
5. Rape, Abuse & Incest National Network
Why Will Only 3 Out of Every 100 Rapists Serve Time?
6. Time March 2010
Sexual Assaults on Female Soldiers: Don't Ask, Don't Tell
7. Time March 2014
It's Time To End Rape Culture Hysteria.

Unions And Voting Rights
1. Cornell University Online
 The 1911 Triangle Shirtwaist Fire
2. Wikipedia
Louis Waldman
3. Wikipedia
The Radium Girls
4. The New York Times December 2012
Bangladesh Finds Gross Negligence in Factory Fire
5. BBC Online October 2013
Bangladesh Clothing Factory Hit By Deadly Fire
6. BernieSanders.com
Top Ten corporate Tax Avoiders
7. ABC News January 2013
What Veterans May Need More Than a Walmart Job
8. Bloomberg Business Week June 2013
Costco CEO Craig Jelinek Leads the Cheapest, Happiest Company in the World

Texas And The Summer of 2013
1. NPR September 2013
Famous For Filibuster, Wendy Davis To Run For Texas Governor
2. Burnt Orange Report   November 2013
Tea Partiers Continue to Disrespect Women and Latinos, Call Senator Van de Putte "Barrio Boopsie"
3. The Lubbock Avalanche-Journal   July 2013
DPS director responds to letter on security report

Women Have A Message For YOU!
1. Rising Tide blog March 2014
Practically Feminist

www.ingramcontent.com/pod-product-compliance
Lightning Source LLC
Chambersburg PA
CBHW060250290526
45789CB00001B/275